D1279746

Infertility

Other Books in the Social Issues Firsthand Series:

23 ⁹⁶

**SOCIAL ISSUES
FIRSTHAND**

Infertility

Norah Piehl, Book Editor

GREENHAVEN PRESS

An imprint of Thomson Gale, a part of The Thomson Corporation

THOMSON
™
GALE

Detroit • New York • San Francisco • New Haven, Conn. • Waterville, Maine • London

Christine Nasso, *Publisher*
Elizabeth Des Chenes, *Managing Editor*

ISBN-13: 978-0-7377-3839-1 (hardcover)

ISBN-10: 0-7377-3839-1 (hardcover)

Library of Congress Control Number: 2007933970

Contents

Chapter 1: Infertility's Effects on Self and Family

People who have dealt with infertility discuss how the problem has shaped and changed their perceptions of themselves and their relationships.

Chapter 2: High-Tech Solutions

Couples who have used in vitro fertilization (IVF) and other assisted reproductive technologies (ART) explore the procedures, their financial and emotional costs, and the potential side effects of ART, including multiple births.

Chapter 3: Adoption, Surrogacy, Childlessness, and Other Options

Hopeful parents share stories of alternatives to IVF and
other high-tech options, including alternative medicine,
surrogacy, and adoption. Writers who exhausted other
options also discuss accepting infertility, and, in some
cases, childlessness.

Foreword

Social issues are often viewed in abstract terms. Pressing challenges such as poverty, homelessness, and addiction are viewed as problems to be defined and solved. Politicians, social scientists, and other experts engage in debates about the extent of the problems, their causes, and how best to remedy them. Often overlooked in these discussions is the human dimension of the issue. Behind every policy debate over poverty, homelessness, and substance abuse, for example, are real people struggling to make ends meet, to survive life on the streets, and to overcome addiction to drugs and alcohol. Their stories are ubiquitous and compelling. They are the stories of everyday people—perhaps your own family members or friends—and yet they rarely influence the debates taking place in state capitols, the national Congress, or the courts.

The disparity between the public debate and private experience of social issues is well illustrated by looking at the topic of poverty. Each year the U.S. Census Bureau establishes a poverty threshold. A household with an income below the threshold is defined as poor, while a household with an income above the threshold is considered able to live on a basic subsistence level. For example, in 2003 a family of two was considered poor if its income was less than $12,015; a family of four was defined as poor if its income was less than $18,810. Based on this system, the bureau estimates that 35.9 million Americans (12.5 percent of the population) lived below the poverty line in 2003, including 12.9 million children below the age of eighteen.

Commentators disagree about what these statistics mean. Social activists insist that the huge number of officially poor Americans translates into human suffering. Even many families that have incomes above the threshold, they maintain, are likely to be struggling to get by. Other commentators insist that the statistics exaggerate the problem of poverty in the United States. Compared to people in developing countries, they point out, most so-called poor families have a high quality of life. As stated by journalist Fidelis Iyebote, "Cars are owned by 70 percent of 'poor' households. . . . Color televisions belong to 97 percent of the 'poor' [and] videocassette recorders belong to nearly 75 percent. . . . Sixty-four percent have microwave ovens, half own a stereo system, and over a quarter possess an automatic dishwasher."

However, this debate over the poverty threshold and what it means is likely irrelevant to a person living in poverty. Simply put, poor people do not need the government to tell them whether they are poor. They can see it in the stack of bills they cannot pay. They are aware of it when they are forced to choose between paying rent or buying food for their children. They become painfully conscious of it when they lose their homes and are forced to live in their cars or on the streets. Indeed, the written stories of poor people define the meaning of poverty more vividly than a government bureaucracy could ever hope to. Narratives composed by the poor describe losing jobs due to injury or mental illness, depict horrific tales of childhood abuse and spousal violence, recount the loss of friends and family members. They evoke the slipping away of social supports and government assistance, the descent into substance abuse and addiction, the harsh realities of life on the streets. These are the perspectives on poverty that are too often omitted from discussions over the extent of the problem and how to solve it.

Greenhaven Press's Social Issues Firsthand series provides a forum for the often-overlooked human perspectives on society's most divisive topics of debate. Each volume focuses on one social issue and presents a collection of ten to sixteen narratives by those who have had personal involvement with the topic. Extra care has been taken to include a diverse range of perspectives. For example, in the volume on adoption, readers will find the stories of birth parents who have made an adoption plan, adoptive parents, and adoptees themselves. After exposure to these varied points of view, the reader will have a clearer understanding that adoption is an intense, emotional experience full of joyous highs and painful lows for all concerned.

The debate surrounding embryonic stem cell research illustrates the moral and ethical pressure that the public brings to bear on the scientific community. However, while nonexperts often criticize scientists for not considering the potential negative impact of their work, ironically the public's reaction against such discoveries can produce harmful results as well. For example, although the outcry against embryonic stem cell research in the United States has resulted in fewer embryos being destroyed, those with Parkinson's, such as actor Michael J. Fox, have argued that prohibiting the development of new stem cell lines ultimately will prevent a timely cure for the disease that is killing Fox and thousands of others.

Each book in the series contains several features that enhance its usefulness, including an in-depth introduction, an annotated table of contents, bibliographies for further research, a list of organizations to contact, and a thorough index. These elements—combined with the poignant voices of people touched by tragedy and triumph—make the Social Issues Firsthand series a valuable resource for research on today's topics of political discussion.

Introduction

Thanks in part to popular television shows and movies, the idea of a female "biological clock" is a widely accepted part of a woman's aging process. In the television shows "Ally McBeal" and "Sex and the City" and in the comic strip "Cathy," for example, women in their thirties and forties are depicted in a race against time, a countdown until the day when their ovaries stop producing eggs, signaling the end of their fertile years.

Even before that inevitable time comes, though, women are warned that they shouldn't wait too long to have a baby, as doing could have dire consequences. From dramatically decreased fertility (which starts to decline as early as age twenty-seven according to a 2002 study)[1] to increased chances of breast cancer in the mother[2] and Down syndrome in the baby,[3] the risks of waiting too long to start a family are emphasized to women in medical literature and media representations alike. The hazards of bearing a child later in life are so well documented that at many hospitals, mothers over thirty-five have their files labeled "AMA" for "advanced maternal age," signaling their high-risk status to medical personnel.[4]

Until very recently, however, the conventional wisdom has been that men remain as capable of fathering a child at seventy as they were at twenty. Aided by images of high-profile celebrities such as actor Michael Douglas, broadcaster Larry King, and late night talk show host David Letterman having children (with much younger wives) into their sixties and seventies, men have traditionally felt confident in their ability to put off childrearing as long as desired. Several new studies, however, have suggested that for men, delaying parenthood holds just as many risks as it does for women.

Infertility—It's Not Always the Woman's Problem

Despite evidence to the contrary, for many years doctors and hopeful couples assumed that if a couple was having trouble conceiving, the failure was due to a medical problem with the woman. According to urologist Dr. Harry Fisch, author of *The Male Biological Clock* (2005), however, "in about 40 percent of these [infertile] couples the problem lies with the man. In another 40 percent, it's the woman with the problem, and in another 20 percent either both partners contribute or the cause is unknown." Despite these statistics, however, Fisch notes that some fertility clinics have historically failed to perform thorough semen analyses to assess male fertility, instead focusing all attention on the woman.

Unlike women, who may experience years of physical symptoms—such as hot flashes and infrequent or irregular menstrual periods—that might indicate declining fertility, men rarely have any physical signs of decreasing fertility. Writer and editor Kevin Chappell notes in *Ebony* (June 2005) that unlike a woman's biological clock, a man's "doesn't strike at midnight, signaling an absolute end to fertility. It's more of a gradual process with testosterone levels declining with age." Nevertheless, according to recent studies, men over thirty-five are twice as likely to struggle with infertility as men twenty-five or under.

Other Risks Come to Light

According to a 2004 article in the *Journal of the American Medical Association* by science news reporter Paul D. Thacker, the links between a man's age and genetic mutations in his sperm—and resulting birth detects in offspring—have been known since the 1950s. Researchers have now found at least twenty different disorders that correlate with paternal age. These include higher incidents of achondroplasia (a type of dwarfism) and several types of cancer among the offspring of older fathers. What's more, according to Fisch, recent studies have suggested that half the cases of Down syndrome in offspring of women over thirty-five may actually be linked to a defect in the sperm of the father.

New evidence also links higher rates of schizophrenia and autism to the age of the father at the time of conception. Writer Roni Rabin reports that, in a recent study, "children of men who became a father at 40 or older were 5.75 times as likely to have an autism disorder as those whose fathers were younger than 30." These new studies have led many to wonder whether skyrocketing rates of autism among children are due, at least in part, to the trend of both women *and* men delaying childrearing until their thirties and beyond.

Unlike women, who are born with all the egg cells they will ever produce, men produce new sperm cells throughout their lifetimes. For a long time, it was assumed that these newly generated cells were immune from deterioration as a man aged. The germ cells that produce sperm, however, undergo cell division through mitosis approximately every sixteen days—a total of 380 divisions by the time a man reaches thirty and 610 divisions by age forty. As Thacker writes in *JAMA*, "each round of division creates another opportunity for an error." Compare these figures to the germ cells that produce a female's eggs, which undergo a total of only about twenty-four divisions, and it's clear that men may contribute at least as many opportunities for genetic mutation in their offspring as women do.

A Sense of Shame

If scientists have known for years about these links between a father's age and infertility, why has it taken so long for this information to be made available to the public, particularly to couples struggling with infertility? Part of the problem, according to journalist Judy Foreman, is that unlike prenatal tests such as amniocentesis and ultrasound, which often detect large-scale chromosomal errors linked to defects in the egg, the types of smaller genetic mutations caused by aging or defective sperm are very difficult to test for.[5]

Another reason that issues surrounding male infertility have rarely come to light is the mistaken connection between fertility and virility or masculinity. There's a sense of shame connected with male infertility that is perpetuated by embarrassing, often demeaning diagnosis and treatment methods. Writer Patti Hartigan gives the example of a male friend undergoing fertility treatments, who "complained that he had a better relationship with a specimen cup than he had with his wife."[6] A contributing editor for *Babytalk* magazine Geoff Williams, upon finding out that his low testosterone level was responsible for a failure to conceive, writes, "In an out-of-body experience, I then watched my male ego walk across the room, open the second-story window, and jump out."[7] Perhaps recent media coverage of the links between advanced paternal age and fertility complications will help revise the image of older celebrity male role models fathering babies. Other celebrities, such as champion cyclist Lance Armstrong, whose children were the product of sperm he froze prior to undergoing chemotherapy for testicular cancer, are already helping bring male fertility problems out of the closet.

Time to Wake Up

In the media, female characters in books and movies have an emotional response to their ticking biological clocks, bemoaning the little time they have left to start a family. Perhaps the public's new awareness that male fertility also declines with age will encourage men, as well, to think more deeply about the passage of time and their own desire to start a family. Kevin Courtney, a writer who had previously reveled in his emotional immaturity, grudgingly admits that "we've been denying [the biological clock's] existence for so long, it's become buried deep inside us, and probably needs a good dig with a stiletto heel to bring it back to the surface."[8]

Author Amy Sohn writes that, in New York City at least, men in their thirties are beginning to view fatherhood as desirable, even enviable. She writes of "Maclarenism" (the male yearning for high-end, high-tech strollers) and of a man who found himself browsing cribs at a local furniture store just months after beginning a romantic relationship.[9] Perhaps, if Sohn's anecdotal evidence is accurate, more men are beginning to take these new data to heart, to learn to listen to the alarm of their biological clocks instead of just hitting the snooze button.

Notes

1. Cited in Carl T. Hall, "Study Speeds Up Biological Clocks," *San Francisco Chronicle*, April 30, 2002, p. A1.
2. National Cancer Institute Breast Cancer Risk Assessment tool, www.cancer.gov/bcrisktool.
3. Cited in National Institutes of Health, "Facts About Down Syndrome," www.nichd.nih.gov/publications/pubs/downsyndrome.cfm.
4. Roni Rabin, "It Seems the Fertility Clock Ticks for Men, Too," *New York Times*, February 27, 2007, p. Fl.
5. Judy Foreman, "Men Have a Biological Clock, Too," www.myhealthsense.com/F010703_biologicalClock.html.
6. Patti Hartigan, "The 'Male Factor,'" *Boston Globe Magazine*, June 18, 2006. p. 16.
7. Geoff Williams, "What a Man!" *Baby Talk*, October 2006, p. 70.
8. Kevin Courtney, "Pregnant Pause," *Irish Times*, May 11, 2002, p 51.
9. Amy Sohn, "Watching the Clock," *New York*, May 2, 2005.

SOCIAL ISSUES
FIRSTHAND

CHAPTER 1

Infertility's Effects on Self and Family

I Just Want to Be a Dad

Michael Snider

For as long as he can remember, Michael Snider's ideas about his future have included having children someday. Even when he was a teenager, he wrote and daydreamed about what his future children would be like and about what kind of father he would be.

Now, though, in his early thirties, Snider is being forced to deal with the possibility that his imagined future might not include children. He and his wife, Tammy, have spent nearly four years unsuccessfully trying to conceive a child. Their efforts to find a medical basis for their infertility have been fruitless.

Snider's essay poignantly expresses the heartbreak infertility can cause, particularly when individuals view the possibility of parenthood as an integral component of their identities. It also underscores the importance of remaining optimistic in the face of ongoing disappointments and at times embarrassing procedures.

Michael Snider is a researcher and reporter for Maclean's *magazine.*

I always figured I'd be a father by the time I was thirty. I know I'd be a good one, too. Growing up, I always preferred to hang out with the kids—regardless if it was my younger cousin or a squad of neighbourhood children. I still do, actually. (OK, probably because I'm still a bit of a kid myself.) But I'm two years past that thirty year mark now and not a dad—though certainly not by choice. It turns out my wife Tammy and I are victims of some cruel trick of nature, because despite wanting nothing greater out of life than children to raise, there's been no drug, technique, or sage advice that has brought us any closer to our goal.

Well, so far, at least. We still hold out hope, but we get more anxious with every month that ticks by. I've discovered that being unable to conceive a child is the most depressing thing a couple can face.

Starting to Try

We started trying soon after we were married in 1999. A year later, after switching to boxer shorts, trying new techniques and (at least pretending) to "just let things happen," we spoke to our family doctor, who referred us to another doctor who referred us to another doctor. In some ways, it would be easier if they found something that medically disqualified us from having kids. Then, we could just get on with adoption rather than go through more frustration. But no: we're part of that 20 per cent of couples whose infertility is unexplained.

We started with a prescription for a drug called Clomiphene. It tricks the brain into thinking the ovaries are slacking off. After a year, we moved to Gonal F, which I would inject into the tissue around Tammy's stomach. (That was fun: a spot of blood popped up once and I nearly passed out.) Gonal F is supposed to stimulate egg production and carried a 25-percent chance of multiple pregnancies. We joked that we would publish a request for names for our sixteen children.

But no luck. It's always the same: the anticipation builds up during the final two weeks of the cycle, and we're carefully pessimistic—if it doesn't work again, we won't have too far to fall. Like most couples, we handle disappointment differently. My wife needs comfort, attention, and talk. I withdraw, stave off bouts of blinding fury, and want desperately to *fix it*.

Once, after another negative test, we rented a tearjerker about a father dying of cancer who tries to reconnect with his son by building a house together. Hey, good choice: already emotionally zapped, we watched the film with rivers of tears streaming down our faces and ended up doubled over on our green leather couch laughing at the absurdity of it all. One thing about experiencing disappointment is it gets a little easier each time to handle. We've learned that the trick is to stick together, and if laughing at each other blubbering over a movie helps, then so be it. That's what we'll do.

Unfading Resolve

But even with our troubles, I never question our resolve to have kids, mostly because of our niece, Madeline. When my little brother walked out of the hospital room with her, he wore a smile radiating with wonder. She's almost three now, beautiful and very smart. Every once in a while, she'll spend the day with us and run circles through the house while we play "scare me": kitchen, dining room, living room ... *BOO!* Kitchen, dining room, living room ... *BOO!* She has this way of all of a sudden saying or doing something that fills me with this alien flush of happiness that I'm sure fathers experience all the time. Just little things like, one afternoon, we were eating Jello and I was doing something to make her laugh. In the midst of an infectious giggle she sputtered, "*Uuuncle Mii-ike.*" That's all it takes. Another time, while I was absorbed in a World Series game, Maddle suddenly appeared at my chair and banded me a huge birthday card marked with bright crayons. My control was exemplary: I fought off a flash of red heat to my face and gave her a big hug.

A Long-Held Dream

I used to keep a diary in my teenage years, when keeping a diary seemed like such a necessary part of understanding life and understanding who you are. Sometimes I'd catch myself writing to my as yet unborn child and imagine that one day this unnamed, yet somehow tangible figure would be moving boxes in the basement and come across the pages I had written. I'd picture him or her reading about dad and taking lessons from his experiences. I think about the lessons my father taught me—hold the door for people behind you, respect your mother, don't try and pull the curve ball, take it to right field—and want to pass them on.

My worst fear is of finding myself old and grey one day with no memory of holding my child for the first time, of watching game-winning home runs, meeting first boyfriends, crying at weddings. Will I consider my life unfulfilled, maybe even wasted? What fond memories will I have to look back on? My dedicated years of work, the oak entertainment centre I built, the time I barbequed that steak perfectly? Just not the same thing.

I kissed my wife goodnight about an hour and a half after celebrating the arrival of the New Year. We talked about our hopes for the coming year. She admitted she almost started crying at about five minutes to midnight, when the thought struck her that, a year from now, nothing may have changed. We hugged each other and promised—once again—that we'd try and think about it in a positive way. I turned out the light and lay beside her, and thought, for the millionth time, how much I want to be a dad.

I Feel Like a Failure

Rachel Giese

Rachel Giese knew that being a lesbian wouldn't conflict with her dreams of becoming a mother. She imagined that with modern artificial insemination techniques, becoming pregnant would be a relatively easy process. But when Giese and her partner, Jenn, started trying to have a baby, their efforts lasted months and resulted in frustration, stress, and feelings of failure for Giese.

Here Giese, in addition to describing the various medical procedures she underwent, also honestly expresses the bitter pain that results from infertility: the feelings of inadequacy, the sense of resentment toward pregnant friends, and the bitterness and cynicism felt toward well-meaning folks who say "everything happens for a reason." Giese's essay also conveys the common seesaw thoughts shared by many who struggle with infertility, as they swing between overwhelming feelings of hopelessness and the thought that such despair is purely selfish. Giese's writing is honest and raw, as the author admits to being angry and volatile rather than simply suffering in silence.

Rachel Giese is a writer and columnist for the Toronto Sun *newspaper. Following publication of this essay, Giese and her partner decided to adopt a son, now three years old.*

The first hot flash struck at a party, the happy occasion of the opening of a new arts centre for street kids, full of drumming demonstrations and store-bought hummus, bright paintings on the walls, and the goaty smell of excited teenagers.

I had been warned to expect hot flashes at any time, but for the first few, claustrophobic moments I thought I was hav-

Rachel Giese, "What Unbearable Means," *This Magazine*, January–February 2004.

ing a panic attack. One minute, I was chatting happily with a friend, the next I was suffocating, sick from the smell and the noise of the room. I was gripped by a cold, shivery clamminess as sweat evaporated off my burning skin. My internal thermometer careened up and down trying to control my body temperature. My brain still worked, barking out simple commands—Sit down. Take sweater off. Drink water. Breathe—but the rest of me was stumbly and slow to follow direction. The glass shook in my hand. My head got stuck in my turtleneck. My lungs didn't seem to work. Then it was over. Passed as quickly as it arrived, leaving me jelly-kneed and drenched.

Thanks to clomiphene citrate—better known by the brand names Serophene and Clomid—I was in the throes of menopause at the age of thirty-three. Clomid acts on the hypothalamus to set the process of ovulation and estrogen production in motion. Clomid is cheap and effective. It's the wonder drug of infertility treatment, and one of the reasons the number of multiple births has increased over the past two decades in North America. Clomid twins and triplets, I called them. Even one would be enough to me. For sixteen months, I had been trying unsuccessfully to conceive. My doctor hoped the drug would at last jumpstart my sluggish ovaries.

As I mopped myself up, I spotted a woman across the room, a friend of a friend. She, too, had tried for a long time to have a child. Six years, I'd been told. In her arms, she was holding her fat, laughing baby. See that, I told myself. Maybe miracles do happen.

Motherhood Dreams

I had always imagined I'd be a mother. Growing up, my dreams alternated between becoming a jet-setting writer with homes in Paris and New York or a life-saving doctor caring for refugees in some far-flung war zone. But always, there'd be kids. Three or four of them—I can still see the offspring of my childhood fantasies so clearly—crawling adorably under-foot. There was a husband too, but he was always blurry and indistinct. A bland, neutered Ken to my glamourous, pink Corvette–driving Barbie.

When I came out as a lesbian at the age of twenty, I barely missed a beat. It was 1990. I knew a handful of lesbians and gay men who had kids, either from previous marriages or some combination of reproductive technology and adoption. It was the beginning of what would soon be cutely dubbed the gayby boom. Resources and support groups for gay parents ware springing up all over. At twenty, I could barely look after myself, let alone a child, but when the time came there would be sperm banks and friendly social workers to ensure my dream came true.

Eight years later, I fell in love with a woman who, among her many wonderful qualities, wanted to be a parent, too. At the start of our relationship, we planned to have a family and decided that I should be the one to get pregnant. Jenn had a permanent, well-paying job with benefits, while my freelance work was less lucrative, less stable, and more easily interruptible by a pregnancy. Plus, I was four years older than Jenn and already in my late twenties. For me, it was soon or never.

Putting the Pieces in Place

The only question was the other half of the equation. We wanted our child to know his or her father and to have some kind of relationship with him, but we didn't want the potential complications of raising a kid with a third party. It was a struggle to find the right fit, until a friend (let's call him Kevin), in whom we had been confiding about our desire to have a baby, made us a generous offer. His sperm was ours. No strings attached.

Within two months, he and I were tested for sexually transmitted diseases and genetic abnormalities. I started monitoring my temperature each morning to pinpoint the exact time of ovulation. Our friendly gay doctor gave us advice for low-tech, home conception and tossed in some syringes for the insemination. (Contrary to the popular myth, turkey basters are too big and unwieldy.)

Of course, I assumed I'd get pregnant right away. My [menstrual] periods are as consistent and regular as a Swiss-made watch. I'm obnoxiously healthy. Tall, big-boned, with childbearing hips. My peasant ancestors gave birth in the fields in the morning and were back on their feet in time to make cabbage mils for dinner.

In our excitement, we told everyone we knew we were trying. Our first attempt was scheduled for December 20, 2001.

Then, one week before, we received what felt like a benediction. Friends of ours, a couple who had been trying to have a baby for a year and a half, announced they were pregnant. We had been terrified that we would get pregnant before them, worried about the enormous guilt we'd feel. But they were expecting. We were in the clear.

Early Disappointments

On January 1, 2002, I woke up hangover-free. Nothing stronger than soda water had crossed my lips the night before. I went to the bathroom to pee and it was then that I noticed my period had arrived.

Happy New Year.

We tried fourteen times over the next twelve months, growing more frantic and despondent with each failed cycle. I spent hours on the Internet researching fertility treatments. I ingested herbs and vitamins, quit caffeine, subjected myself to acupuncture sessions, and, on the advice of a practitioner of Chinese medicine, ate bushels of squash and yams to make my uterus a more accommodating environment.

We varied our insemination routine: one month, three days in a row; the next, every other day over six days. For an hour after Jenn withdrew the syringe, I'd lie with my bum perched up on five pillows, willing the sperm a speedy journey to my fallopian tubes. After our first few candlelit attempts, we gave up trying to make our DIY-baby-making romantic. Six months or so into trying, Jenn was inseminating me while we watched Law & Order reruns.

Vicious Cycles

For that year, this is how we lived: from the end of my period to the time we inseminated we were caught up in a giddy excitement, when we'd discuss baby names and plan for the future. Then for the next two weeks, we'd wait anxiously for the start (or we hoped not) of my period. To pass the time, we'd pick fights with each other and fret. I would obsess over every perceived symptom. Was that a cramp? Is my skin breaking out? Are my breasts usually this tender? I'd race to the bathroom hundreds of times a day to check my underwear for spotting. Finally, my period would come and we'd fall apart, usually in our own private corners. Jenn would withdraw and I would rage. We'd let each other cry. We'd resent every pregnant woman we saw on the street and be knocked off our feet each time someone announced they were having a baby. Sometimes even the sight of a happy parent with a baby or toddler would cripple us. Then, after a few days of blinding grief and self-pity, the cycle would start all over again.

When I think back on the first three years of our relationship, before I began trying to get pregnant, it seems so slight by comparison. Meeting, falling in love, fighting and making up, growing to trust each other, learning how to communicate, moving in together, coping with losing a job (me), and helping a best friend move to the other side of the world (Jenn). Those experiences, so significant at the time, forged our relationship, but as we struggled to get pregnant, I felt like an absolute amateur. Nothing had prepared us for this. Infertility had become the defining experience of our relationship, against which everything else would be compared. Jenn lost her mother to cancer the summer we met—only that, she says, was more agonizing than trying month after month to become parents and failing each time.

A Haunting Kind of Need

For me, I'd never experienced anything so traumatic. Though I had always wanted a child, the desire had largely been intellectual. Suddenly, a new roaring, visceral need overwhelmed me. I was amazed by my hunger for a baby, my craving for the smell of their heads and the weight of them in my arms. It was as though as soon as I started trying some dormant animal response kicked in, compelling me to keep going, despite the mounting evidence that I might not ever be able to conceive and despite the toll the cycle of hope and disappointment was taking on our lives.

My unrealized children haunted me. I'd see people on the street—toddlers and adults—whose features might be an amalgam of Kevin's and mine and I'd ache with maternal longing: That person could be my child, at five, or ten, or twenty. At night, I dreamed I had babies, but then lost them, leaving them behind in elevators, or subway cars, like a mislaid pair of gloves.

One rainy day I saw a woman pushing a stroller with a clear plastic hood. I looked inside, but instead of a child the woman was pushing along a little dog dressed in a snowsuit. It was so absurd, so deeply weird that I burst out laughing, but it terrified me too. Was she just an eccentric, coddling dog lover? Or was I looking at some manifestation of myself—someone whose frustrated parenting energy would soon be channelled in creepy directions?

Seeking a Specialist

By August, I was certain something serious was wrong. I badgered our family doctor to find me a specialist. He insisted it was too early. He sent me for blood tests and an ultrasound and Kevin for a semen analysis. We passed with flying colours.

"See," he said, "you just need to relax and be patient. It will happen." I continued to press him, finally striking a deal. If I wasn't pregnant by Christmas, he'd refer me to a fertility doctor.

In February 2003, I had my first appointment with Dr. B, a smart, soft-spoken but steely doctor who believed in aggressive therapy and high-tech treatment, which I found comforting. No crystal-rubbing earth goddess in Birkenstocks was going to get me pregnant with herbal tea and affirmations. Dr. B, with her arsenal of hormones, ultrasounds, catheters, and petri dishes offered us our best chance of having a child.

I may have been lousy at getting pregnant, but I was an excellent infertility patient. I read all the books I could find on the subject, researched treatments on the internet, showed up early for all my appointments.

When another round of tests all came back normal, Dr B began to suspect that the problem was ovulatory. Usually there are twelve to sixteen days between ovulation and the beginning of menstruation; this gives a fertilized egg adequate time to implant into the uterine lining. My luteal phase lasted only ten days. To correct it, Dr. B suggested fertility drugs and cycle monitoring, which meant going to the clinic at seven o'clock in the morning six or seven times a month to measure the fluctuations of my hormones and the development of my follicles, which house eggs.

Monitoring My Cycle

Cycle monitoring is as unpleasant as it sounds: getting up before dawn to have blood drawn by a groggy lab technician and your insides poked at by an internal ultrasound probe. Sometimes as many as twenty-five women would be at the clinic for monitoring. Try as they might to be friendly and personal, the nurses couldn't help us from feeling like we were a herd of cattle being sent for studding services. One particularly tense morning, when charts went missing, the doctor was late and a nervous lab tech had botched half of our blood tests, one patient cracked up the silent waiting room by letting out a low, drawn-out "mooooo."

The doctors and nurses kept the collective tsunami of grief and anxiety dammed with a professional, upbeat distance. There was excellent medical advice and care, but very little coddling. Some cycles, my treatment was altered several times, with little opportunity for consultation and discussion, as the doctors measured my daily hormone levels and follicular development, tuning my reproductive organs like a piano. Whatever control I still thought I had over my body was gone. I resented the invasiveness of the tests, the unpredictability of the drugs, the way monitoring took over my life. Still, after more than a year of overexamining my body's every twitch and secretion, second-guessing everything I consumed, and blaming myself for every failed attempt, I was more than happy to hand myself over to the experts.

Renewed Hopes

Progesterone supplements failed. Clomid failed. I moved on to Puregon—a powerful injectible follicle stimulant that I learned to shoot into my belly each morning with the finesse of a junkie. After three unsuccessful cycles, Puregon finally worked, almost too well, blowing up my normally almond-sized ovaries to the size of oranges and producing thirteen eggs.

Without any warning, I was hustled over to the in vitro fertilization team and three days later my eggs were retrieved and fertilized in a petri dish with Kevin's sperm. Five days later, two perfect embryos were transferred to my uterus. We were no longer guardedly optimistic, we were, at last, truly hopeful.

Three days before my pregnancy test was scheduled, I noticed a pinkish spot in my underpants. By the end of the day, it was heavier, like a period. I called the clinic, frantic with worry. The nurse reassured me that bleeding in early pregnancy was normal, but told me to come in early for the test anyway. Later that day, she left a message with the test results.

"I'm so, so sorry," she said. "I'm so, so sorry."

The True Meaning of "Unbearable"

Suffering might make some people saints, but it made me bitter, volatile, and inconsolable. To borrow a line from Anne Lamott, I felt as though Jenn and I had been exiled from the ordinary world—where people just had kids when they wanted them and everything turned out okay—to the Land of the F---ed, a vast, ugly desert with vultures flying overhead and the two of us with blisters and sunburns and never enough water. And to make matters worse, everyone else seemed to be living it up and sipping fruity drinks in a shady cabana.

Several friends had conceived and given birth since we started trying. We struggled to be happy for them, while we grieved for ourselves. Before this, I had used the word "unbearable" to describe tight shoes and bad television. Going through infertility, I knew what it really meant. Some days, I couldn't stand being in my own skin, didn't know how I could bear to take another breath, felt like the pain and disappointment would never end.

Sometimes, something would snap me out of my overwhelming sorrow—a television documentary about a refugee camp, full of hunger and disease and despair—and I'd think to myself, "Who do you think you are? How dare you feel sorry for yourself?" But mostly, I was prickly and wounded, holding myself and others to an impossibly high standard. Picking at Jenn, shutting out my friends, bristling at people who tried to offer support, but seething with resentment at those who didn't come through.

"Everything Just Happens"

"Everything happens for a reason." A year and a half into trying to conceive, I'd heard this so many times I wanted to scream. People believe this—conservatives and progressives, atheists and the religious. My Catholic grandmother would have called it God's will. What surprised me, though, is how many of the people around us believed this. Intellectual, political people deeply committed to the possibility of change just seemed to give up in the face of The Big Mystery. In the end, we were all chess pieces being moved by some unseen hand to some predestined fate.

"Everything happens for a reason." This is what people would say when another pregnancy test came back negative, when another drug protocol failed, when another woman who "wasn't even really trying" would bludgeon us with the news of her pregnancy. It was an attempt at comfort, an attempt to put a meaning to something difficult and painful. But I hated the easy resolution it offered. Hated to have this enormous, consuming experience reduced to a glib adage that could fit inside a Hallmark card. Hated the pull-up-your-socks tone of it. Hated that in the midst of what felt like the sky falling down, I should look for meaning and find comfort in the notion that this was my destiny.

But there was no solace in trying to understand why this had happened to us. Sorrow is meaningful, but what causes it is often senseless, random, and unfair. Cars crash. Tumors metastasize. Babies don't get born. This was the hardest thing to ask of myself and other people: to let this just be terrible. To let us just be deeply, bitterly sad and angry. To let there be no comfort. Because everything doesn't happen for a reason. Everything just happens.

No Happy Ending

This is where there should be a happy ending. It's time to reveal that I did, in the end, get pregnant. With twins. Or that we recently adopted a child, who is gorgeous and healthy, and sleeping on my lap as I write this. That hasn't happened. Not yet. We are taking a short break from trying, to allow my body to heal itself, but really to give us time to figure out what to do next.

There was a happy ending, though, of a different kind. It was this: slowly, it began to hurt less. There was no epiphany, just a quiet realization that it wasn't as hard as it used to be. The wound was still there, and probably always would be, but it was no longer raw and open. Partly, it was our growing resolve that we would not go on like this forever, that this path was coming to an end. Partly, I think, I was just cried out and raged out and tired of being miserable. I hadn't found a reason for what we went through, and doubted I ever would, but I had found compassion and gratitude, feelings I had had in very short supply for two years. For our friends and family. For Kevin and his kindness. For Jenn and her courage. For the good fortune that is so easily taken for granted: health, a comfortable home, interesting work. And like the recovery from a long illness, there was such relief and lightness in just feeling something close to normal again.

Why Can't I Have Another Baby?

Brett Paesel

Secondary infertility is defined as the inability to conceive a child following one or more successful pregnancies. In this essay, Brett Paesel uses matter-of-fact humor to shed light on this common, but little-discussed, problem.

Brett Paesel views motherhood with a combination of sarcasm and joy. When her son Spence was almost three, Paesel, then in her early forties, became obsessed with having a second child. After a year of trying, Paesel and her husband saw her doctor to see if there was an explanation for the couple's secondary infertility.

Here Paesel describes that doctor's appointment, including her secret fantasies about what might be causing her infertility, her dismay that her aging eggs might be to blame, and her growing hopefulness, fueled by her doctor's optimism, that she and her husband might still conceive. In the end, Paesel reveals that her longing for a second child stems more from her concerns over her son's future than it does from any personal motivation or desire.

Shortly after writing this article and initiating the adoption process, the author did *find out she was pregnant with a second child. Brett Paesel is an actress and writer living in Los Angeles. Her humorous book,* Mommies Who Drink, *was published in 2006.*

I HAVE A THREE-YEAR-OLD SON, and I've come to the conclusion that raising a young child involves long stretches of boredom interrupted by flashes of terror and bursts of supernatural joy—which sounds awfully close to the definition of psychosis. And, also, I am told, combat. One would think that, knowing this, I would send my child off to boarding school and surgically ensure that I never have another child. But no. For a reason I cannot name, I am obsessed with having a second one.

For a year, I pee on all kinds of sticks. Sticks that tell me when I'm ovulating. Sticks that tell me if I'm pregnant. I get crazy about sticks. I buy them in bulk and pee on them even when I'm not ovulating or remotely close to being pregnant. I begin to live by the sticks.

I circle the best days in my date book for getting it on. I wake Pat in the middle of the night for sex. Because the stick says *now*. Then I lie on my back with my legs propped against the wall until they lose all feeling and fall onto the bed. I wake Pat again, pounding my paralytic legs with my fists.

I read adoption books and daydream about flying to India to pick up a little girl. I even talk to someone who has a baby connection in Nigeria. But I back out when I realize that we communicate only through his beeper and pay phones.

A year of this and no success. I am desperate—driven by a force beyond myself, like [actor] Richard Dreyfuss in [the movie] *Close Encounters of the Third Kind*. So I decided to have my doctor run some tests that will tell me a little more about my chances of getting pregnant.

The day I go in for the results of the tests, I wait alone in the lobby. Pat and my son park the car while I sit on a brown leather sectional [sofa] and start to finger the neatly placed magazines on the glass table in front of me. I consider reading the article on "Ten Things Men Would Like Us to Know." But I'm not sure I want to know. I look up to see bamboo shoots in a glossy green pot on the corner of the table. Behind them is a painting of the Buddha done by my doctor, Dr. Sammy. He is a Buddhist, which is and is not a good thing in an obstetrician. At his best, he is cool, detached, and amused. At his worst, he is cool, detached, and amused.

When I was looking for a gynecologist, I asked a couple of friends for their recommendations. The first said that she had a great doctor: thorough, no nonsense. "It's just . . ."

"What?" I said.

"Well, it's silly, really. It's just that he has no sense of humor."

"I don't know that that would matter," I said.

"Well, then, he's your man," she said. "It's just that one time he was doing a Pap. I mean he was right in the middle of it. My feet are in the stirrups. And the lights go out all over the hospital. And he just . . ."

"What?"

"Well, he waited until they came on again. He didn't say anything. Nothing to break the tension. I lay there in the dark, my legs spread, and listened to him breathing, while the greasy speculum slipped out of me."

"What happened?" I asked.

"The lights came on. And he finished the job. He just went on like nothing had happened."

Not sure about that, I thought.

My next friend said that she had a great guy she had known for years. He was practically a friend.

"It's just . . ."

"What?" I said.

"Well, his sense of humor is a little strange. It's okay with me. But you might not like it."

"Like what does he say?"

"Well, the last time I was making an appointment with him he said, 'Great, I can't wait to see that luscious bod. I'll be waiting, with my tongue hanging out.'"

"Ewww."

"He was just joking."

Not my guy, I thought.

My next friend said that she had met her gynecologist in acting class. He was a Renaissance man—doctor, painter, actor—and Buddhist.

"It's just . . ."

"What?" I said, weary.

"It's just. Well, he's handsome."

"So what?"

"Well. Some people don't like that in a gynecologist," she said.

"How handsome is he?"

"Very handsome," she said. "He played the Devil in a scene for acting class. And he was so sexy that the women couldn't take their eyes off him."

"Your gynecologist played the Devil?"

"He was good," she said.

Pat and Spence join me in Dr. Sammy's office. I look out the window and see sky clean as a blue sheet, sunlight bouncing off white squares of concrete in the street below, glinting cars maneuvering in a parking lot. I try to imagine Dr. Sammy as the Devil, and my mind skids to a short list of things I'd be willing to trade my soul for.

"So let me see here," he says.

I hear him open a file, but I keep my attention on the sheet sky. Spence climbs into my lap.

"He's three now?" Dr. Sammy asks.

I think, *Get to it, get to it. What does the file say?*

"Almost three," says Pat.

"I've got some stickers," says Dr. Sammy. He pops out of his reclining chair and sprints out of the room.

Spence squirms off my lap and on to Pat's.

Is he stalling? I wonder. *Are the stickers a delaying tactic while he gets up the nerve to say that while getting information about my fertility status, he found out that I'm riddled with cancer? It's a brain tumor, I'm sure. I'm always sure it's a brain tumor. Wait a minute—he didn't go anywhere near my brain. It would have to be ovarian cancer.* I see myself six months from now wearing a turban, looking thin and impossibly beautiful, being wheeled into Spence's preschool graduation ceremony.

Dr. Sammy bounces back in with stickers and hands them to Spence.

"Stickers!" Spence says, sliding off Pat's lap onto the carpet.

Dr. Sammy plops down in his chair, grabs the file, and leans back again.

I see Pat in my hospital room, moving the tubes aside, and carefully lying down next to my waif-like body. Hanging onto my last few breaths, I whisper, "I loved only you."

"Your progesterone is good," says Dr. Sammy.

Pat looks at me, smiles, and grabs my hand like we won something. It's not cancer.

"Pat's sperm is good."

Pat nods like he knew that all along.

I look down to see Spence sitting in the middle of all the frog stickers he's stuck to the carpet. He looks up at me and smiles. King Frog with his subjects.

"So what is it?" I ask.

"Well, Brett, it's nothing really," says Dr. Sammy. "It's just that you're forty-two and your eggs are old."

"But I don't look like I'm forty-two," I say. "Forty is the new thirty."

A patient smile spreads across his face. "Not biologically," he says.

I realize at this moment that I hate him.

"Old eggs?" asks Pat.

"Mmm," says Dr. Sammy, leaning forward, his beaky nose hanging over his weak mouth. "A woman has only a set number of eggs at birth. She loses these eggs as she gets older, and by forty, the eggs that remain are old. They're tired."

How old are they? I hear in my head. *So old they need a walker just to get over to the uterine wall.*

He goes on, "There's a higher risk of chromosomal problems. And it's harder to get pregnant." I watch as he rests his talons on top of the file.

"Christie Brinkley had a baby at forty-four," I say.

"I'm not saying you can't get pregnant," he says. "In fact, if I were to bet on a forty-two-year-old getting pregnant, I would bet on you."

"You would?" I ask. My voice sounds girly and flirtatious, not my own.

"You've got everything going for you," Dr. Sammy says. "You've got the blood pressure of a teenager."

"I do?" I ask, giggling.

"And your uterus is in great shape. Pink and healthy."

"Pink. Great," I say.

Dr. Sammy is such a handsome, kind man, I think. *We should have him over for dinner sometime.*

Spence grabs onto my knee and pulls himself up from the frogs. Pat raises an eyebrow at me and turns to Dr. Sammy. "Well we wanted to know what we're dealing with because if it looks unlikely that we'll get pregnant, we're going to start looking into adoption," he says.

Spence pulls on the neck of my shirt. "I want more stickers."

"Just a minute," I say, prying his fingers away. "Dr. Sammy's talking to Mommy."

Dr. Sammy laughs.

"Well, that's a sure-fire way to get pregnant—start adoption proceedings."

"Really?" I ask. I look at Dr. Sammy's lovely, long fingers.

"Stickers," says Spence, his voice insistent.

Pat reaches over and touches Spence's hair.

"Just a minute," I hiss. "So why would starting to adopt make me pregnant?"

"Well, it's nothing scientific, right?" he says, winking at Pat. "It's just the way the world works. You get what you want when you're looking the other way."

"STICKERS," screams Spence.

"Spence," I say. "This is my turn. I get to talk to the doctor now. You are not the only person in the world."

Spence's face drops and he sinks back to the carpet of frogs.

My heart lunges toward him. I want to take it back.

I want to say, "You *are* the only person in the world. That's the problem. That's why we're here. I'm terrified that you will be alone some day. I can't sleep, thinking of you alone in the world." The truth of this hits me like a hokey God moment in a made-for-TV movie.

I hear Dr. Sammy intone more about my pink cervix and attractive follicles. I hear percentages and terms like "artificial insemination" and "donor egg."

But most of this sounds like it's bits and pieces from outside a door. Inside, I hold my answer. Turn it over and tuck it into my chest. My answer. The reason for this near-psychotic pining for a second child.

The reason offers itself up and I know that it's been there since the day my brother was born. It is this: I want for my child what I have. A witness. Someone who will say, "Yes, it's true. Yes, I was there. We were so very loved."

Infertility Strengthened My Family

Jacqueline Bodnar

Jacqueline Bodnar views her long struggle with infertility with a great deal of optimism. In hindsight (now that Bodnar and her husband have children), Bodnar credits their infertility battles with many positive aspects of their marriage and family life.

For example, Bodnar credits the entire process with bringing her and her husband closer together as they worked toward a common goal. She also explains that she became more mature, more ready to have a child during the long years of waiting. She took the time to make parenthood the top priority in her life, re-defining her career goals and readying herself to become a wonderful mother. All these things would not have been possible, Bodnar argues, if she and her husband had been able to get pregnant right away.

Jacqueline Bodnar and her husband dealt with unexplained infertility for five years before Bodnar gave birth to a girl in 2004 and a boy in 2006. Bodnar is a freelance writer who lives with her family in Daytona Beach, Florida.

Struggling through five long painful years of infertility isn't something that most people would look back upon and actually be thankful for. Then again, I'm not like most people. I don't know what it's like to have an unplanned pregnancy or to get pregnant when trying to conceive for a short time. No, I've always taken the long road. I've always taken a little longer to accomplish things, and pregnancy was no different.

I was ready to start having children about two years before my husband was ready. Then when we were both on the same page and ready to start trying for a baby, we never imagined

Jacqueline Bodnar, "How Infertility Made Me a Better Mom," americanbaby.com. May 20, 2005. Reproduced by permission of the author.

what would happen. Month after month went by and we couldn't conceive. Before I knew it, two years of trying went by. Then I went to the doctor to see if there was something wrong.

Doctor Visits Begin

The first gynecologist did a series of tests to rule out all kinds of possible reasons for the infertility. Some tests were painful, while others were embarrassing. They found nothing wrong so I went home and kept on trying each month. After another year went by I went to another doctor and went through some tests only to once again be told that everything seemed normal and healthy.

The next logical step was to make sure everything was up to snuff with my husband. Again nothing was found to be abnormal. So we started watching the calendar, using ovulation kits, reading, crying, and thinking. We looked into going to an infertility specialist but found that the cost of the procedures were way out of our budget.

Perhaps the most important thing that happened through those five years of struggling with infertility is how my husband and I grew. We grew as a couple and as individuals and like the saying goes, what didn't kill us made us stronger.

Parenthood Realizations

A lot can happen between the time you are twenty-six and ready to try for a baby and thirty-three when you finally give birth. At age twenty-six, I was ready to become a mother but I didn't have a strong appreciation for parenthood. It seemed to me like just the next step in our marriage. Giving birth to the next generation seemed like something that was expected of me. I thought I had it all planned out when it came to motherhood. I figured I would have the baby, go right back to work, and live the life of having it all.

As the years went on I began to see parenthood differently. I started to really appreciate the idea of getting the privilege to raise a child. I longed so much for the opportunity to get to be a part of the club that only parents are allowed into. I wondered if other parents knew just how lucky they were.

Through this long struggle my thoughts started to change and I began thinking of how I could mold my career into something that would give me more time with my child, should I ever be given the opportunity to have one.

Exploring Other Options

Those feelings became stronger and more concrete over the years. I had accepted the fact that my husband and I were infertile for unexplained reasons. We knew we would have to become parents through other means so we began researching adoption.

Anyone who is trying to get pregnant knows firsthand how many pregnancy tests one can go through. I felt like I owned stock in E.P.T. [a home pregnancy test] For years, at the first sign of a late period or bout of not feeling well, I crossed my fingers and ran to take a test, only to be disappointed.

Then one February morning as we were getting ready to go on vacation I took a test. For the first time ever it read positive. I was beside myself and immediately began to think that it must be faulty. Of course I took about a dozen more tests within the next couple of days, all of which came back positive. Then I had it confirmed by my doctor. I was six weeks pregnant after trying and being ready for so long.

It's Time!

I began to plan and prepare for that magical day and immediately my career aspirations went to the back burner. I began to feel as though the meaning behind having it all was being a mother and wife and having a family. On September 21, 2004, I had an unplanned C-section and gave birth to a healthy baby girl.

For most parents the first weeks that follow are so tiresome and stressful that they sometimes question what they have gotten themselves into. Not for me. I was so happy to have been given the opportunity to have this child that I gladly and without any complaints took care of her at all times. While most parents would dread hearing a 2 A.M. cry, it was music to my ears because each time was a reminder that I was finally a mom.

Long-Awaited Bliss

I don't think for a minute that I would cherish parenthood the way that I do now if I hadn't gone through infertility. I know what it's like to long for a child and not have one and to believe that you may never get the chance to have one.

Those seven years changed who I was as a person and how I look at motherhood. Struggling through years of infertility made me have such a deep appreciation for my daughter and getting the opportunity to be a mother. Today I'm thankful for going through infertility because I truly believe that the struggle has made me a better parent.

CHAPTER 2

High-Tech Solutions

Waiting for a Miracle

Michael Ryan

Michael Ryan and his wife Doreen had been trying to conceive a child for four years before turning to assisted reproductive technology (ART). A general term for the various medically assisted methods tor achieving pregnancy, ART can include such techniques as intrauterine insemination (IUI) and in vitro fertilization (IVF). Following several failed cycles of IUI, Michael and Doreen were ready to turn to the far more expensive and medically invasive in vitro procedure.

Michael Ryan's essay describes the stresses this procedure placed on him and his wife, from the series of injections and the interminable bed rest to the financial burdens and the relentless roller-coaster ride of hopes and fears. Near the end of this excerpt, the couple discovers that Doreen is pregnant—with four embryos, a development that causes its own set of joys and complications.

Although Michael and Doreen considered the option of performing a fetal reduction to improve the babies' odds of survival, all but one of the fetuses died of natural causes before they had to make that decision. Michael Ryan's full-length memoir of their infertility and his wife's high-risk pregnancy is entitled Baby B. *He is a poet and professor in the English department at the University of California, Irvine.*

Like most couples who one day find themselves in a doctor's office discussing assisted reproductive technology (unironically known as A.R.T.), Doreen and I had always thought that all we had to do in order for her to get pregnant was stop trying not to. Wrong. Doreen did everything but stand on her head afterward. She would jam a pillow under her butt and lie immobile for thirty minutes with her knees tucked and her pelvis tipped up. She used ovulation-predictor kits. "Does this look blue to you?" she'd ask me, holding the plastic stick in front of my nose. She bought a ninety-eight-dollar thermometer to measure the minute spike in body temperature that accompanies ovulation. We also tried: Forget-about-it-and-relax romantic weekends. Herbs. God-awful teas. Diet and exercise. No diet, no exercise. Doing it a lot, doing it a little, this way or that way. Early in mid-cycle. Late in mid-cycle. Exactly at mid-cycle. Abstaining beforehand for two days, three days, four days, five days, one week—a Rubik's cube of permutations.

None of them worked.

Assisted Reproduction Technology

So we tried assisted reproductive technology. Our H.M.O. [health maintenance organization] would cover six intrauterine inseminations (or IUIs, in which the sperm is deposited by catheter into the uterus at ovulation), provided that our primary-care doctor would testify that we had been trying on our own for at least two years. We had actually been trying for four years—almost as long as we had been married. Doreen was thirty-one when we started; she had just turned thirty-five when we began the IUIs. The look on her face when she saw someone else's baby was an unfailing reminder that she felt time running out. She never said anything more than "What a darling little girl." But I knew what she felt. It wasn't that she didn't have a baby. It was that she might never have one.

Over the next fifteen months, we tried nine IUIs, waiting two weeks after each one to find out whether it had worked. With IUIs, the chances of conceiving get worse with each attempt: from one in five-to-fifteen after the first try to about one in a hundred after the sixth. Finally, our doctors began to speak about other options, by which they meant in vitro.

Whereas an IUI is relatively easy and cheap, in vitro is invasive and expensive. But the odds for successful conception are better: one in three for each attempt in women between thirty-five and thirty-seven. After three attempts, three out of five couples achieve a pregnancy.

By now, Doreen was almost thirty-seven and I was almost fifty-three. Neither of us had any children. We were officially among the twenty-five percent of couples over thirty-five classified as infertile—which, we learned, is usually diagnosed after a couple has had one year of unprotected, well-timed intercourse. And so we called Dr. Werlin.

Dr. Werlin

Lawrence Werlin is one of the best reproductive endocrinologists in Southern California. He has been practicing in Orange County since 1982. He sees between forty and forty-five patients a day. He has done more than two thousand in vitro fertilization [IVF] procedures, with a success rate well above the national average, and was selected by his peers as Orange County's Best Doctor in Infertility for the years 2000 and 2001. His clinic is in Irvine, where I teach at the University of California and where Doreen, who is a poet, works from our home. Werlin is about my age, and very much of my generation. He plays Rolling Stones tapes over the speakers in his examining rooms, and recently attended a Stones concert in Las Vegas. Sometimes he sings along with [Stones vocalist] Mick Jagger during sonograms. He could probably hold his own in a mosh pit. He's a big, athletic-looking guy, with a boyish gap between his two front teeth and shoulder-length iron-gray hair, and he dresses in scuffed running shoes and pale-blue surgical scrubs. He is definitely a Personality. The first time he called us, I picked up the phone and a loud voice said, "Hey, Mike, this is the Whirl." "Who?" I asked. He is the Whirl. He moves fast and does shtick with the patients:

"Yo, Doe!" he shouts when he greets Doreen. "You look bee-you-tee-ful!"

"Bless you," Doreen responds politely, as if he had sneezed.

"And there's my man," the Whirl says to me, pumping my hand.

One time he called me Rick and another time Steve; usually he addresses me generically, as "my man." I don't mind. I can't imagine keeping track of as many patients as he does, much less remembering everything he has to about the latest clinical discoveries, drug protocols, and surgical techniques. He runs a multimillion-dollar business that few people could manage for long without burning out; he regularly puts in fourteen-hour days and time on weekends, and is often on call. There is a rigorous maintenance of the upbeat in his manner and throughout his clinic, a public atmosphere encasing the private emotional extremes of cold medical facts: You're pregnant! You aren't. You can have a baby! You can't. When I remarked on this to him, he said he has to "Stay Positive." "I believe that's a big part of this," he said.

I am trying to Stay Positive. Every night at ten, I go into the bathroom to prepare the Gonal-F and Lupron injections that make up the first round of in vitro treatment while Doreen lies in bed, calming herself. She hates needles. Just seeing one makes her heart race. It is her only phobia, as far as I know. Before this cycle of treatment is over, she will have been punctured with needles more than two hundred times. . . .

When I've finished giving both shots, Doreen's eyes open and she says, "Thank you, sweetheart." She says this with no irony. This is her alternative to crying: to think of the other instead of oneself. This is how we are trying to Stay Positive. The Whirl is right: there is no other way to get through this.

Harvest Day

Today is harvest day: retrieval of the eggs. Each egg—a single cell, two-hundredths of an inch in diameter—is drawn into a suction trap as the fluid-filled follicle that contains it empties and collapses. The eggs are incubated, inseminated with sperm, and left in a petri dish for three days, to develop into four-to-eight-cell embryos that will then be shot from a catheter into Doreen's uterus—"Bye-bye, kids! Don't forget to write!" Dr. Werlin's standard procedure for women in their late thirties is to transfer up to six embryos from dish to uterus, risking the chance of a multiple pregnancy in order to maximize the chance of a single pregnancy. (For younger candidates, some specialists incubate the eggs for a longer period of time, and then transfer only one or two embryos.) Despite the sophisticated technology, the procedure is conceptually crude: take an egg out, inject some sperm, wait a couple of days, put the thing back, and see what happens. If an embryo implants itself in the uterine lining, that's a pregnancy. We'll get the results via blood test in two weeks.

Very little is known about how conception actually occurs. The first "test-tube baby" was born in 1978. Since then, the drugs and protocols have changed rapidly. In vitro fertilization, a now common procedure, didn't exist twenty-five years ago, and twenty-five years from now the cutting-edge technology that Dr. Werlin uses may seem like treating colic with doses of black lead. Because IVF is such a new science, the long-term effects associated with it are not fully understood. There are some known risks along the way, though; for example, Gonal-F may cause ovarian hyperstimulation syndrome (OHSS), a complication that can result in death. But the syndrome is very rare. There have been incidents of ovarian cancer in IVF patients, but as yet no relationship between cancer and any of the in vitro drugs has been established. Each woman who undergoes in vitro is implicitly accepting both its known and its unknown risks.

Early Mornings

Since Doreen began the first cycle of in vitro treatment, we have had to go to the clinic every other morning at seven, for blood tests to monitor her FSH [follicle-stimulating hormone] level and ultrasounds to monitor her swelling ovaries. South Orange County is one of the richest areas in the country; many people in the entertainment business move here from Los Angeles when their careers are over, people whose livelihood depended on their appearance. But nobody looks glamorous in Dr. Werlin's waiting room at 7 A.M. All the couples this morning are straight and white, but there are several women by themselves. Some of them are on their second or third round of in vitro, and their conversation is about frustration, failure, and disaster: the dangers of this or that drug, the number of surgeries and ectopic pregnancies and miscarriages they have had. The lucky ones for whom in vitro has resulted in a healthy baby are not here, although occasionally, and surprisingly, there are women with sleepy, subdued children. The children are the stars. We look at them with shameless longing.

Doreen and I head next door to the surgical center, where in an hour Doreen, under anesthesia, will have her eggs harvested and I will be invited to accompany myself into a lab bathroom to "produce a specimen" for the inseminations. I do not particularly feel like producing a specimen. My wife is about to have an operation that entails unconsciousness and intubation. This does not inflame me with desire.

Producing a "Specimen"

But I kiss her goodbye and go to the lab. They present me with a plastic cup and lid in a bag and point me toward the bathroom. I've probably done this fifteen times in the past fifteen months, for IUIs and semen analyses, each time abstaining from sex for three to seven days beforehand—most recently for a sperm sample to be frozen, in case the Birth Partner (me) has what they gently call "a problem" on the day of the retrieval, which is today. The sample is here in the clinic; I imagine it as a little disk, like a Junior Mint without the dark-chocolate coating. There is doubt about the effectiveness of thawed sperm, however; fresh is better. So of course I want fresh. I want to maximize our odds.

But, as it turns out, the Birth Partner does have "a problem." Doreen is in a hospital bed next door and I'm sitting on a toilet with my pants around my ankles. There's a TV and a VCR up on struts near the bathroom ceiling. In the metal closet next to the sink, on the shelf below the Penthouses and Playboys, there are three pornographic videotapes. I have not watched a pornographic movie for years, but since I cannot arouse myself, I pop a tape in the VCR. . . . It is about as erotic as being slammed in the face with a brick.

I switch the VCR off. But I can't afford to give up. If Doreen doesn't get pregnant, I don't want to think it was because my aged sperm were dopey from waking out of a long hibernation. I go outside and ask the lab director how much time I have before the doctors need the specimen. He says one hour. Our home is fifteen minutes away. I stop by Doreen's bed and tell her what happened, and that I am going home to try again. She says I shouldn't worry, we can use the frozen sperm. She is kind, even though I could be jeopardizing our only chance to have a child.

At home, I walk upstairs to our bedroom and climb under the covers of our bed. I close my eyes and breathe deeply, and open them to see the snow-tipped mountains fifty miles away through our bedroom windows. It's March 2nd, a crystalline winter day. "The creature hath a purpose, and its eyes are bright with it". Unaccountably, this line from Keats's letters comes into my head. He meant it critically—as human will interfering with the active receptivity to experience he called negative capability—but I find it comforting at this moment. Everyone else in the world is simply going ahead with their own concerns, whipping up and down the freeways or trudging rutted mountain roads, doing what they do to live.

I drive back to the clinic with my sperm in the plastic cup, lodged in my crotch to keep it warm. I deliver it to the lab attendant with minutes to spare. Doreen is coming out of surgery. When she wakes up, I'm standing by her. She's O.K., she says, just a little woozy, and asks me how I am.

"It worked." I am grinning.

"My hero," she says, and we laugh.

Four Tiny Embryos

One four-cell, one seven-cell, and two eight-cell embryos went into Doreen at ten-forty-five this morning (March 5th). Only these four embryos had successfully fertilized. We have their pictures. They look like mud pies.

The transfer took place in an operating theatre with a cyclopean ceiling light. I stood behind Doreen, facing Werlin. He sat on a stool between her legs, flanked by nurses. A lab technician brought in a catheter loaded with our embryos—a tiny amount of colorless fluid—and asked her, "Are you Doreen Gildroy?" For legal reasons, Doreen had to respond with the full sentence, "Yes, I am Doreen Gildroy." She then initialled the catheter, and the technician handed it to Werlin.

"Here we go, guys," Werlin said. "Just relax, Doreen."

Doreen closed her eyes, to concentrate on her breathing.

"You might feel some pressure now," Werlin said. He guided the catheter—a thin translucent tube—through Doreen's cervix into her uterus. It was the same procedure used for IUIs, but this time there were embryos in the attached syringe, not sperm, and the stakes were immeasurably higher.

"This is it," Werlin said. "Are you O.K., Doreen?"

She said she was.

"All right. Just breathe normally."

A Little Surprise Party

With his right thumb, he gradually depressed the plunger of the syringe. It has been estimated that if you inject the fluid as you normally would, the embryos hit the back of the uterine wall at six hundred miles an hour. The idea is to lay them in there gently—in the end, it all depends on fallible human skill.

Then he was finished. He handed the catheter to the technician, who left for the lab, where it was examined under a microscope to make sure the embryos were not still in it. She was gone for only a minute.

"It's fine," she said.

Then Werlin said to the nurses, "Ready? One. Two. Three."

They all shouted, "Get pregnant, Doreen Gildroy!" It was startling, like a surprise party when the lights go on, and very sweet. Then, after instructing Doreen not to move for thirty minutes, they left us alone. I took her hand.

"I love you," I said.

"I'm trying not to cry," she said. "I don't want to shake the baby out."

"I know," I said. "It's fine. It's all going to be fine." But I had no idea what the disappointment would do to us if she didn't get pregnant. How could I be sure it was all going to be fine? . . .

A Positive Sign

Pregnancy test this morning, waiting for the results. Doreen was shaky on her feet. It was the first time since the transfer that she had walked farther than the bathroom and back to bed. Her hobbling drew some stares from the other women in Werlin's waiting room this morning. It identified her as having made it past the embryo transfer, since you don't go through this series of [intramuscular estrogen] shots otherwise. In other words, it meant she had a chance of being pregnant.

I answered the phone when it rang this afternoon.

"Yo, Mike. The Whirl."

"I know," I said.

"You sitting down?"

"I am."

"Good news, buddy. You have another phone for Doreen?"

Doreen was lying in bed. I told her that it was Werlin. She scanned my face for the news, and read it in a nanosecond.

"Hello?" she said, her face like a thousand-watt bulb.

"You're pregnant, Doreen!" shouted Werlin and a Wagnerian chorus of nurses. There must have been someone on every phone in the clinic. . . .

A Tiny Heartbeat

Sonogram today. . . . It does not take long to find a dot with a pulsing white pinpoint of light.

"Thar she blows!" Werlin shouts. "Bee-you-tee-ful! Look at that heartbeat!" It's beating a hundred and forty times a minute, he tells us.

Doreen cranes her neck, so she can see. I press her hand. The rapidly pulsing pinpoint means life. We are all mesmerized by it, even Werlin and Laurie, who must have seen it thousands of times before.

Laurie keeps moving the probe inside Doreen—side to side, up and down, to sweep the whole uterus—but there's only one pinpoint of light there.

"How about that, guys?" Werlin asks, after he's satisfied that the ultrasound has swept every cubic micrometre. "There's your baby!"

"Just one?" I say to Werlin.

"You'd like a few more?"

"One's fine," I answer. "One's just enough."

"More could possibly show up next week," Werlin says, his tone suddenly sober. "But you've definitely got your one. And it's in the uterus. You can see the strong heartbeat, right there. Ga-boom ga-boom ga-boom. Those are the main things we're looking for today."

Laurie takes a measurement of the embryo, as well as of Doreen's ovaries, which are swollen to the size of avocados from the Gonal-F. Then she prints out some digital snapshots of the dot with the pinpoint of light, and hands one to me.

It's Twins! . . . or More!

There were more showing this week. As soon as Laurie inserted the probe, two dots flashed onto the screen: two sacs, two heartbeats. Werlin shouted, "It's twins!" Then Laurie maneuvered, and to the right of the other two, faintly, another pinpoint morphed out of the darkness, like a minnow surfacing in a lake.

I said, "There's another one."

Werlin swooped his head toward it like a big bird, his nose nearly pasted against the screen. "You're right," he said. "There's three. It's triplets!"

"Oh, my God," Doreen said.

Werlin assigned letters to the embryos, from left to right: Baby A, Baby B, Baby C. He put Doreen on bed rest again. This time it was mandatory. He said there was a long way to go and plenty of time to talk about it; right now we should just go home and try to relax. The expression on Doreen's face was like Mary's in Leonardo's painting of the Annunciation: "I'm pregnant with what?"

Can We Do This?

By the time Doreen was dressed, the word had spread among the nurses and staff. "Congratulations, Papa-Papa-Papa," Janet said when we emerged blinking from the ultrasound room into the glare. Then she grabbed my elbow and whispered, "It's going to be fine."

I must have looked stunned. I am stunned. I am stunned, terrified, and (provisionally) elated. There's no way we can do this. We don't have family here to help, we don't have enough money, our house isn't big enough, we can't afford a bigger one. Before it had become obvious that we'd be lucky to have one child, we sometimes thought we'd like to have three—but spaced two years apart, not two minutes. Yet I want to try to do it.

Doreen, resituated in bed, listened patiently to me talk through all this. A triplet pregnancy poses health risks for mother and babies; the more babies, the harder it is to bring them to term. Doreen is the one whose body has to undergo this, plus six more weeks of shots and a third trimester of bed rest. When I had finished talking, she said, "I want to have these babies if possible." That encapsulated my feelings in one sentence. . . .

Too Many?

What a grievous turn this has taken—there are four embryos now. Baby C has become Baby C and Baby D: identical twins. We had just managed to accept the idea of triplets, and now we have quadruplets. As risky as triplets are, quadruplets are exponentially riskier. The health risks skyrocket for both mother and babies. It's not just a question of another baby to care for—as large as that question might be. Doreen is in bed, in shock, with the blinds closed. It seems like an evil fairy tale, where you get too much of what you wish for.

An Impossible Decision

Werlin called with the blood levels: They're fine. "Don't worry," he said. "It's gonna be great." I did not say, "What the hell could you be talking about?" I admit I was not Staying Positive at this moment. He did tone down abruptly when I asked him about the optimum time for a "reduction:" eleven weeks. That's the euphemism—reduction. A needle is inserted through the mother's abdomen into the embryo, injecting a small amount of potassium chloride to cause a cardiac arrest, and poof—that's it. Werlin reminded me that we may be spared this painful experience. Eleven weeks is twenty days away; a whole lot can change in that time. Twenty days ago, we thought Doreen was pregnant with one baby.

Some people would have the babies no matter what. Others, given the medical risks, might feel little compunction about eliminating one or more of them. But the embryos are all alive, and it makes me shiver to think of choosing which is to be killed. The smallest and weakest? Would the twins have a better chance, or the ones in their own sacs? What if you kill some and the remaining ones die later?

I don't know how you make such a decision until there's no more time not to make it. In the meantime, my job is the same: to help Doreen as much as possible and bring her food. She has to have her progesterone and estradiol valerate shots tonight, no matter how she feels. . . . The only thing to do now is wait. I'm clear about what I want. I want Doreen alive and well. But it's her body and, in the end, her decision.

The Truth About Life with Triplets

Cole Moreton

For better or for worse, one of the most common side effects of in vitro fertilization techniques, wherein several embryos are transferred to a woman's uterus, is the possibility of multiple births. For many couples, like journalist Cole Moreton and his wife, the pendulum of infertility quickly swings to the other extreme, as people who previously thought they couldn't have children end up having two, three, or even more.

Moreton's essay is largely humorous in tone, as he reflects on everything he and his wife have given up since the birth of their toddler-aged triplets. He mourns the lack of sleep, the loss of meaningful conversation between spouses, the disappearance of their carefree pre-triplet lifestyle. But, on the other hand, he acknowledges feeling guilty for indulging in these feelings when so many other couples never have the opportunity for even one child. He also reflects on the increasingly common use of fetal "reduction" (selective abortion of one or more fetuses to reduce incidence of higher-order multiples), and comments that, knowing and loving their triplets, he and his wife can't even imagine having used that option.

Cole Moreton is a journalist and editor whose books include My Father Was a Hero *and* Hungry for Home. *He is the deputy editor of the British newspaper* The Independent on Sunday.

Sleep is the new crack cocaine. It's the new wine, the new tobacco. Sleep, sadly, is the new sex. It's what you think about and talk about and crave when you are the new parents of one, two, three beautiful, bouncing, crying, shitting, screaming babies. Sleep is your light at the end of the tunnel. The takeaway can go cold, the bottle unopened, because the bed is waiting, all soft and snug, at the end of a long day that has required the strength, co-ordination, and concentration of a plate spinner swapping his porcelain for three live cats.

Coshed over the head by sleep, at last, you wake 10 minutes later to the sound of crying. The stop-start cycle of exhausted-belly-flop-into-bed-and-dazed-return-to-the-babies has begun. They don't wake all at once—that would be too easy—but one after the other, as if those cute gurgles had been negotiating a hideous rota [list, roster]. But it's OK, the dawn is coming. Daylight will be here soon. And the whole thing will start again.

Which is why the latest findings from Harvard Medical School will have prompted hysterical laughter from the parents of twins, triplets and quads. Researchers interviewed 300 mothers who had had multiple births and compared their lives with those of 128 mothers who had only one child. All the women had conceived as a result of fertility treatment, were educated to degree level, and—according to Harvard—were wealthy enough to cope with the cost of having so many children simultaneously. And guess what the study found? Multiple births were linked to "significant social risks." The mothers were more likely to be depressed and less satisfied with their partners and their home life. Their quality of life was much lower and they felt less secure about their abilities as a mother. Many even questioned the wisdom of having gone for IVF [in vitro fertilization]. Fancy that! How on earth, we wonder, as our befuddled hands pour the porridge into the bin and the contents of the nappies into three bowls, and we try to remember the name of the partner we haven't had a chance to talk to, uninterrupted, for days now, and whom we argue with every time we do steal a moment because the time pressure is so great and we're just not relaxed, how can we be, what the hell do you expect . . . sorry . . . how on earth can anyone regret having triplets?

Let's get one thing straight before we go any further: I know there will be people reading this who have experienced the agonies of childlessness and who would give anything in the world to swap. I remember the pain of that and feel deeply for anyone who is going through it. You have the right to call us self-indulgent whiners who got lucky and must live with the consequences. And that is what makes the bewildering first year of triplet parenthood all the harder. You feel guilty for struggling, guilty for not being able to cope, because wasn't this what you hoped and prayed and nearly bankrupted yourself for? So you keep your mouth shut, don't tell anyone your nerves are frayed, your patience exhausted, your temper explosive. And when you find yourself squeezing that crying baby too hard, or thinking—just for a moment—about throwing it across the room, you remember that it's all your fault, you're the failure, the one who can't cope, the one who gets weepy every time someone says congratulations.

That is how we both felt in those first six months, when whoever was on duty and lying on the sofa cushions next to three tiny Moses baskets on the living-room floor would get an hour's sleep a night—but we never said. When I finally found the courage to tell her I couldn't cope, that I resented these bloody babies and what they were doing to our lives and had to leave or I would go mad, she looked at me in that cool, sane way she has and said: "I know. I feel the same. What gives you more right to leave than me?" Neither of us left.

"Women are destined to carry one child; not twins or triplets or quadruplets," said Alison Cook of the Human Fertilisation and Embryology Authority (HFEA) when the Harvard study was announced last week. "These results show that multiple births are not good for the mother or the children, and any way that we can reduce them without disadvantaging a woman's chances of getting pregnant should be considered."

No mention of the father there, you'll notice. It's true that my own part in family life pales in comparison with the gargantuan efforts of Mrs Moreton, but still ... maybe in Ms Cook's world the men come home in macs [waterproof rain-coats] and trilbies [fedora-like hats] at six o'clock expecting dinner on the table, then go down the pub for a game of darts. Not in mine.

The HFEA, which regulates fertility treatment in this coun-try [United Kingdom], is consulting doctors, patients, and consumer groups about whether to allow just a single embryo at a time to be transferred back into a prospective mother. Two years ago the HFEA revised its code of practice to make it two embryos rather than three, which resulted in a slight drop in the number of multiple births. Our children were conceived just before the change. We wanted three embryos tucked back into Rachel's womb because—like every other couple undergoing IVF—we had absolutely no expectations it would work. The more the merrier, we thought, ignoring the warnings. The news that it was triplets was a shock, a terrify-ing one. How would we cope? But we also had to respond to the doctor who had offered us what he called "reduction." Af-ter years of treatment it is hard to imagine anyone accepting that. Which one would we have lost: Ruby, Joshua, or Grace?

From the moment the nurses carried a procession of wrig-gling human beings from the production line that was my wife, the madness began. Eighteen nappies a day. More than 4,000 bottles in the first year (breastfeeding had to be aban-doned when they got chickenpox). The health visitor shook her head in wonderment, then asked: "Do you have any help?"

Yes, we said. Granny and Nanny live nearby and will be lending a hand. We had no idea just how hard the grandpar-ents would have to work and how much we were asking of them. The health visitor smiled with some relief and ticked a box. Our chance of help had gone.

Later, struggling, we pleaded with various healthcare pro-fessionals and to social services. There was no chance. There was no funding. Someone said social services would not help unless you had quads (a national policy confirmed when we moved town). The attitude was constant, if usually unspoken: you got yourself into this mess with the IVF. If you can afford treatment, you can afford a nanny.

That's rubbish, of course. Even if you haven't spent all your money on doctors and drugs, then clothes and food cost a fortune, so do beds and toys and car seats in triplicate, and every trip out is an expensive expedition, but I won't bang on about this because although it is a struggle—and we had to leave London to afford a big enough house—we are managing. There are others out there doing all this without a reasonable wage, for whom we have huge admiration. Let's just say that a new triplet buggy costs upwards of pounds 600 [about $1,200 in U.S. dollars]. We got ours for much less through the excellent Twins and Multiple Births Association [Tamba]. But here's the thing that outrages Tamba members: the Government promises an extra allowance for the first new child in a family, but if you have two or three at the same time you only get that payment for the first.

Enough complaints. We have learnt to cherish the good moments and forget the bad ones. We have learnt to be quick-tongued as well, on countless occasions when somebody has stood right in front of me triple buggy and asked: "Are they triplets?"

"No," is a good response. "We stole one of them." That foxes people.

Have we both been depressed? Yes, dangerously so in my case for a brief unbearable time. But that was followed by a (belated) realisation that the babies were real, unreturnable, and ours. After that first awful year it got better. It is still hard but (and I never thought I would say this) sometimes—often—it is even fun. I love them. And you haven't been cuddled until you've been cuddled—and dribbled and bounced on and giggled at—by three toddlers all at once.

The Price of Multiples

Sarah Bernard and Hugo Lindgren

Like many couples, Sarah Bernard and Hugo Lindgren assumed that parenthood would be part of their life's plan. But, when conception failed to happen naturally, this high-achieving couple chose to pursue in vitro fertilization (IVF). They knew that multiple births are a risk of the procedure, but still found themselves confused and conflicted when they discovered Sarah was pregnant with twins following their first IVF procedure.

As journalists, both Sarah and Hugo devoted themselves to discovering more about life with twins as they expected a set of their own. Even as they researched, they were dealing with their own twin dilemmas—a health scare with one of the fetuses led their doctor to discuss the increasingly popular procedure of fetal reduction as one possible option. Their essay dwells at length on the ethical implications of this procedure.

Bernard and Lindgren's article balances traditional reporting with emotional, firsthand experience, as the two veteran writers used the time while their infant daughters were in the neonatal intensive care unit (NICU) to write down the thoughts, feelings, and impressions that were the basis of this article.

Hugo Lindgren is the editorial director of New York *magazine. His wife, Sarah Bernard, is a contributing editor for the magazine.*

Two fuzzy heartbeats—our doctor pointed to the black-and-white monitor of the ultrasound machine, and we both squinted and pretended to see what he was talking about. *A lima bean,* we thought, *with a smaller lima bean next to it?* Sensing that we weren't getting it, he punched a few keys and suddenly the small exam room at Cornell's Center for Reproductive Medicine and Infertility filled with a rapid-fire *thump-thump-thump-thump*: our embryos on speakerphone. So wait, it had worked? Twice? When we still didn't say anything, our other doctor piped up: "This is good news, you guys."

How did we feel? Relieved, more than anything, that we didn't have to face starting all over again with fertility injections. And then . . . shocked that there were, in fact, two of them in there. Given that we'd done in vitro fertilization (IVF), twins were a predictable outcome. But we hadn't allowed ourselves to believe it would actually happen.

When we decided to get pregnant, we had imagined a far simpler scenario. We had expected to control the process the way we thought we controlled everything else in our tidy yuppie lives. We felt happily married. We had pretty good jobs. We had a new apartment with an extra bedroom. Having a kid was the natural next step. In a sense, we were merely being swept up in the generational tide, but we also genuinely envied our friends with kids and liked being around them. This is what we wanted.

For ten years, Sarah had, via the [birth control] Pill, put her reproductive system on hold, assuming that it would resume normal service when she wanted it to, right on cue. Which it didn't. One minute, we were enjoying the freedom of our new married life; the next, Sarah was piling ovulation test kits on the counter at Duane Reade [pharmacy] and being told by the woman behind her, just trying to be helpful, that Sam's Club sells them by the case. God help us if we needed that many.

Not as Simple as We'd Thought

Sarah had just turned thirty-one. There was no reason to panic. Until, that is, getting pregnant just wouldn't happen. As the months slid by, the clichés swallowed us up. The terror of feeling you're doomed to never have a child. The good life you'd been living suddenly seeming pointless, a waste. The self-pity. The voice-mail messages from friends calling to catch up and saying, "Oh, by the way, I have some great news." That made us feel jealous and angry, then angry and pathetic for feeling jealous and angry. It got to the point where Sarah started to feel envious of friends who'd had abortions—because at least they knew their bodies were capable of becoming pregnant.

Our evenings at home collapsed into a variation on this theme: Sarah emerging from the bathroom clutching yet another failed test and then us sitting there in stony silence on the bed, watching *Oprah* [TV show] reruns. What would Oprah do? She'd probably be more patient, let it ride for another six months, and relax, take a vacation. But we were beyond the point of being able to enjoy a margarita and a suntan. We needed to reassert control over our lives, and we couldn't wait. So we took our vacation money and went to see Dr. Isaac Kligman at Cornell, a fertility specialist who had been highly recommended to us by Sarah's OB/GYN [obstetrician/gynecologist]. He led us through three rounds of intrauterine insemination (IUI), which set us back about $2,500 a pop, and then IVF, which ran us about $15,000. We organized our lives around the regular morning visits to the clinic and the scary injections. (We'd developed a tag-team approach; Sarah closed her eyes and jammed the needle in, then Hugo pushed the plunger.)

Sarah had two embryos implanted, praying that one would develop into a pregnancy and then a beautiful baby.

A Good Sign?

Within a matter of days, she blew up like a human balloon. Before we had the chance to take the pregnancy test, she'd gained twenty-five pounds so rapidly it was as if we could see her body expanding in real time. Instead of going on the head-clearing weekend away that we'd planned, Sarah was admitted to the hospital. She had "hyperstimulated" from the

IVF medication, an unusual reaction that left her simultaneously bloated and dehydrated. This could only mean failure, we figured.

Our doctors had a different interpretation. This disaster, they suggested, was more likely a positive sign. Doubly positive, in fact. It wasn't just the fertility medications that caused it. It was a high concentration of Beta-HCG, the pregnancy hormone.

Then we saw the heartbeats—the two heartbeats—and we were given an index-card-size printout of the ultrasound as a parting gift. As the news sunk in, part of us wanted to jump up and down, burst into song, embrace total strangers. Twins, holy shit! But, assuming those lima beans could be trusted, did we really want to have two at once? It's hard enough to be the parent of a single baby. Did we have any idea what two would do to us? We decided to find out by immersing ourselves in the parallel universe of multiples, while we still had time.

Surprising Statistics

Like everyone else, we'd noticed the explosion in twins—who could miss those SUV-of-the-sidewalk strollers, with the parents asleep at the wheel?—and understood that fertility treatments were behind it. But that was about all we knew.

The natural odds for twins, we learned, is one pair per ninety live births. But nature's rules no longer apply. The twinning rate has doubled nationally over the past two decades, owing mostly to IUI and IVF, as well as the rising average age of pregnant women (the older you are, the more eggs you release). The city's Department of Health found that the wealthier Manhattan neighborhoods have rates as high as 8 percent. But within social circles like ours, where most of the women are in their mid-to-late thirties, it practically seems like a 50-50 split. We can count five couples we know reasonably well who are expecting right now; two of them are having twins.

For women who undergo successful fertility treatments, the rate of multiples is about one in three. But it seems higher too. A friend of ours who just had twins remembers visiting a fertility specialist and examining his trophy wall of baby pictures. "I was like, 'Cool, there's a set of twins. And there's twins. And . . .' It was all twins!". . .

An Eye-Opening Dinner

To see what we were in for, we invited ourselves over to dinner at Bart and Elizabeth's, acquaintances of ours who live in Tribeca with their 3-year-old twin boys. They also invited their friends Jacob and Alice, who have their own set. (To achieve maximum candor, we agreed to refer here to the grown-ups by their middle names.) The scene there looked idyllic. By 8 P.M., three toddlers in bathrobes, their hair damp from a communal bath, were sitting peacefully on the sofa with their sippee cups, absorbed in *Dora the Explorer*. The fourth was nearby, eating a floret of broccoli without having been bribed to do so and looking adorable in an Elmer's Glue T-shirt.

The grown-ups, meanwhile, sat at a dinner table drinking a bottle of red wine and eating takeout from Odeon. All are in their mid-thirties to early forties, work in arts-related fields, and, in the typical New York way, had experienced most of their adulthood as extended adolescence. They spent their money on dinner and clothes, went to movies, and saw rock bands. Then they decided to start families.

Both Elizabeth and Alice went through multiple rounds of fertility treatments. Both were overjoyed to be having any babies at all and happily embraced the news of twins. And both admit that the blissful scene at the apartment tonight, with four chilled-out kids, is 100 percent anomalous. In the months following the birth of their boys, Bart says, he and Elizabeth experienced "white-hot isolation." Living in New York, he imagined they'd be the people arriving at rock shows with their kid in a sling. "But there was no way," he says. "You know, I'd imagined what it would be like to be the president of the United States and to be an astronaut, but somehow it never came on my list to be a father of twins."

Something They'd Never Imagined

"Oh, it was so beyond anything I'd imagined," says Alice. "On the one hand, it's unbelievable joy and it's everything you wanted and you wanted so badly to have these kids. But I was just remembering those moments where it's Saturday morning and you've each slept about half an hour a couple of times during the night and you're each holding an upset baby and you say, 'Can I give you both babies so I can brush my teeth?' And your husband's like, 'No, I've been waiting for two hours to make the coffee,' and you're like, 'Well, can I just take my puked-on shirt off?!' And he's like, 'No! I have to pee.' And you know that there's, like, fifteen hours ahead of you before bedtime where nobody's going to get sleep again."

For a moment, no one at the table says anything.

Multiples put considerable strain on a marriage. "Basically, the wife hates the husband," says Jacob. Alice cuts in: "You say to your husband, 'Why can't you save me from this? Why aren't you helping me?'" It doesn't matter how much the husband might be helping. Or think he's helping.

"It's what all first-time parents feel," says Elizabeth, "but more." . . .

A "Data-Driven Pregnancy"

Carrying multiples is an endurance test, psychologically and physically. The risk of pre-term labor hangs over you all the time. You get big, really big. The maternity clothes Sarah bought at twelve weeks were painfully snug by twenty weeks.

At twenty-four weeks, strangers in elevators would blithely ask, "Any day now, huh?" (She's become incredibly careful about what she says to strangers in elevators.) Terri Edersheim, her high-risk obstetrician, had forbid exercise of any kind. Even light arm weights, Edersheim argued, would increase her uterine activity and possibly cause contractions, a very bad idea. A cute pregnancy full of prenatal yoga and high heels became another fantasy that Sarah had to let go of.

So we had what you could call a data-driven pregnancy. We went in for a million ultrasounds. We took every test. Edersheim even sent us to Boston to see a 3-D [three-dimensional] ultrasound specialist whom she considers the best in the business. In addition to creeping us out with images of our precious babies looking like space aliens, this ultrasound yielded two important pieces of information. First, it confirmed that we were having two girls; at a previous ultrasound, a technician said it looked that way to her but it was too early to be sure. For whatever reason, that was the one combination we hadn't considered, and it was hard to absorb at first. It wasn't that we didn't want two girls—we just never thought that's what we'd get.

The other news had much more serious implications: Baby B had a "soft marker" for a deadly chromosomal disorder called trisomi 18. That necessitated a trip to a genetic counselor back in New York who walked us through a bewildering array of scenarios that included a "reduction" of the pregnancy to a singleton.

Learning About Reduction

We'd never heard the term *reduction*, but as we looked into it, we discovered that it's become a major feature of the techno-fertility process. When women come out of IUI or IVF more pregnant than they want to be, they see a practitioner like Mark I. Evans, a 54-year-old obstetrician and geneticist who works out of a townhouse in the East Sixties. Though he's been doing this for more than twenty years, he still has a cowboy mentality. "We do some pretty bizarre shit," he says. "I've seen women pregnant with septuplets, octuplets. My record is twelve."

Back in the early eighties, when Evans was a young professor at the Wayne State Medical School in Detroit, he thought he knew how to stop the heart of a single fetus without harming any others in the womb. It involved an injection of highly concentrated potassium chloride. He didn't use it on a human patient until he received a call from a physician treating a four-foot-ten woman pregnant with quadruplets. The doctor had recommended to her that she get an abortion, but having spent seven years trying to get pregnant, she asked if there was such a thing as "half an abortion." Evans thought he could do that for her, and when he did, his medical career began its strange odyssey to the present day. "I turned those four into two, and they're out of college already," he says. "Then I got a call from a lady in Alaska who had octuplets. She was a little taller, but even King Kong couldn't carry octuplets. So we turned her into two, and those kids are in college. By now, I've done thousands of patients."

On the day we went to his office, Evans was wearing aquagreen scrubs and a nice gold watch. On the wall, he had pictures of himself with talkshow host Phil Donahue, broadcast journalist Diane Sawyer, and, of all people, Pope John Paul II. Evans sees himself as a crusader for the cause of rational family planning. "Our goal—and here's your sound bite—is healthy families," he says. "It doesn't matter how many. When I first started this thing, nobody except for the most fundamentalist of folks had a problem reducing four or more, because the outcomes were so horrible." he says. "So the ethical debate was triplets. People were claiming, 'Oh, you don't reduce triplets, they do so great.' But the data doesn't support that. The average gestational age is three weeks earlier than twins, and the perinatal mortality rate is considerably higher."

Over the years, as three-to-two reductions became routine for Evans, he slowly approached a new threshold. What about going all the way down to one? He'd done it, of course, but only out of medical necessity. Now, he admits, it had become "more a matter of lifestyle. The typical story is, second marriage for both, he's got two kids from his marriage, she's got two from hers, they just want one of their own."

Reduction: Ethical Limits

Two years ago, the feminist Amy Richards told *The New York Times Magazine* about her decision to reduce the triplets she was carrying. She rejected the option of twins as still too much of an imposition and health risk and had her doctor reduce her pregnancy to a single fetus. Predictably, she was excoriated by right-to-lifers. What was more surprising was the relatively conflicted reaction she received from the pro-choice side. A decision like hers made people uncomfortable, like a kind of yuppie eugenics.

Even the freewheeling Evans tones down his rhetoric when he explains his decision to do the two-to-one procedure. "When you start doing anything radically new, you start with the life-and-death situations," he says. "You start with the nothing-to-lose cases. As with every technology, as the risks and benefits get better known, those indications liberalize. I came to the ethical conclusion that if you believe that one-to-zero is ever acceptable—i.e., that a woman should be allowed to have an abortion—then why not two-to-one? I came to believe it was a valid choice."

Fewer and fewer are likely to be put in that position, though. IVF technology is improving to the point where doctors can better identify the hardier embryos so they don't have to stack the deck by implanting more than one. "We're almost at the point where we can consider single-embryo transfers," says Jamie Grifo, head of the reproductive-medicine program at NYU Medical Center. "The Europeans are already doing that. But you can't always control the process even then. I had a patient who was terrified of having twins. So I said fine, and we put in one embryo. Guess what? [It] split. She got twins."

As for us, reduction ceased to be a consideration as soon as we did an amniocentesis test and it came back clean. But the brutal little detour had an unintended benefit. The fear of losing one brought us to terms with how intensely we wanted both of our little girls. . . .

It's Time

Everything's fine and then suddenly everything gets complicated. At week thirty-two Sarah goes in for a routine stress test that shows no signs of contractions. She comes home, makes herself dinner, sits down to watch *The O.C.* (the prom episode [of the TV show]) with her friend Ondine, and her water breaks. They say there is no mistaking it, and that is true. Ondine goes running downstairs to fetch Hugo from the gym; he sees her blonde head coming through the gym door and he knows instantly what must be happening. Ondine hails us a cab. We rush to New York Hospital, where the contractions start coming hard and fast. Sarah asks everybody who looks like they might be a doctor or a nurse why this is happening. What had she done wrong? Should she not have made dinner? She wants an explanation.

Baby A's head is pointing south, in the proper position, but Baby B is lying east-west, which puts her at risk of breech [presentation of the fetus buttocks first instead of head down]. So we're going Cesarean. Sarah is convinced we didn't make it long enough and that our girls are in danger.

They give her an epidural, load her on a gurney, and wheel her into the operating room. She is still asking for an explanation as the doctors swab her stomach and a nurse covers her arms with a blanket. The procedure goes quickly. Hearing a few muted cries, Sarah wants to know, "Do they look like babies?" Hugo peers around the curtain that blocks Sarah's view of her own insides, but all he can see are one baby's feet. "The feet look good," he tells her. "Not too tiny." The weights are announced: Baby A, a.k.a. Scarlett, is three pounds, fourteen ounces; Baby B, a.k.a. Orly, is four pounds, two and a half ounces.

The Tide Turns

Our lives go into slow motion. The girls are taken to the NICU [neonatal intensive care unit], where they are placed in clear plastic incubators called Isolettes, while Sarah recovers in a hospital room upstairs. Being in this situation was our biggest fear all along, the situation of the babies' being not okay. We thought if we did everything right—if we did the injections properly, if Sarah rested and ate well and rested some more—then we could will them into existence. When the nurse takes Scarlett out of her Isolette and lets Sarah hold her for the first time, the numbness that enabled Sarah to climb out of her hospital bed is broken by how terrible she feels that our little girl has to go through this alone.

And then, over the next few days, it all starts to turn. Though we are allowed to stay with them as long as we wish—and can feed them and change them and bathe them—we are largely spectators to their incredible resurgence. Scarlett and Orly are upgraded to the "feeders and growers" category, advanced placement in the NICU. We watch with pride as four-pound Scarlett requires two nurses to hold her little arms down so they can get her IV back in. One day we arrive at the NICU to find our girls reunited in a single incubator. In baggy white kimono undershirts, they've both rolled to the inside so that their foreheads are touching. It is clear that somehow they are giving comfort to each other, and all that distress and worry we had been hoarding over the last two years washes away. How could we have ever had less than these two?

A month goes by, slowly, and then we get a couple of days' notice that the girls are well enough to go home. We surprise ourselves by not freaking out. Yet. As we write this, they are coming through the door.

CHAPTER 3

Adoption, Surrogacy, Childlessness, and Other Options

After Traveling the World to Use Donor Eggs, We Adopted

Suz Redfearn

The cost of in vitro fertilization, egg donation, and other high-tech reproductive methods put these options out of the range of many middle-class Americans. Many, however, are pursuing these procedures in other countries, where the costs are not so prohibitive. It's a phenomenon known as "reproductive tourism," and it's what Suz Redfearn and her husband Marty did after exhausting their life's savings on expensive in vitro procedures that failed to result in a pregnancy.

Suz and Marty traveled to Capetown, South Africa, where a well-known, highly successful doctor offers egg donation and in vitro fertilization services at a fraction of what the cost would be in an American fertility clinic. What Suz and Marty realized in advance after much researching, however, is that this lower-cost option may also result in lower rates of successful pregnancies.

To their surprise, though, Suz and Marty did find themselves parents despite a disappointing foray into reproductive tourism. Although Suz had always rejected the idea of adoption, when a real-life possibility arose, the couple figured they had nothing to lose. Thanks to a young woman in South Carolina, Suz Redfearn was finally able to consider herself a mother, and even found it surprisingly easy to come to terms with having a baby without having a pregnancy.

Suz Redfearn writes about health and travel. In addition to writing regularly for the Washington Post, *her work has appeared in Salon.com, Slate.com and* Men's Health.

I first heard about the charismatic Paul le Roux after my third In Vitro Fertilization [IVF] attempt failed. My eggs, it seemed, were shot. Yet, at thirty-nine, I just couldn't seem to walk away from my intense desire to give birth.

With my husband Marty's acquiescence, I began looking into the world of donor eggs, which pairs the ova of another woman—selected for her youth, health and often her education and looks—with your partner's sperm in a petri dish. The resulting embryos are transferred to the uterus of the woman trying to get pregnant. The intended mom (me) loses her genetic connection to the child, but the man (Marty) doesn't, and you still get to experience pregnancy.

As far I was concerned, donor eggs were a mighty appealing option, except for the cost: $30,000 per attempt, with about a 50 percent success rate. Undoable for us, especially as we'd already spent more than $70,000 over the past five years on everything from IVF to acupuncture to expensive dietary supplements—none of it covered by health insurance. We were, after all, just a couple of Washington-area reporters with unimpressive salaries. We'd already plowed through some inheritance, accepted a family loan, plundered our savings, and racked up credit-card debt. Yowza. We couldn't do much more unless we found a more affordable way.

Reproductive Tourism

Enter le Roux, a South African fertility specialist with a devoted following in the United States. I discovered his name on an online bulletin board for women with faulty eggs, where anonymous infertiles were chatting excitedly about escaping the high prices in the United States by jetting overseas.

In what has been dubbed reproductive tourism, these women were flying all over the place: Argentina, Ukraine, Mexico, Greece, Spain and, most appealing to me, South Africa, where le Roux had helped a number of them get pregnant. His patients raved about how kind he was, how involved, compared with American reproductive endocrinologists, who more often than not are in a big hurry and are unwilling to do the hand-holding craved by those stuck in the grief-filled pit of infertility. Not so with le Roux, apparently. From what the women online said, he was the man.

The cost of his services? About $5,000. In the United States, that same $5,000 would pay only the donor's fee. And that doesn't include any medical services. Of course, we'd have to fly 8,700 miles across two hemispheres and six time zones to get to Cape Town and spend two weeks in a hotel there, which would run us $4,000 to $6,000. And, if we wanted to be able to see pictures of our egg donor as an adult and possibly even meet her, we'd have to use the one donor-egg agency that operates in Cape Town and is run by a Californian charging U.S. prices ($4,500). Or we could go with le Roux's donor pool (baby pictures of the donor only, no chance of a meeting).

Total out of pocket? About $14,500 if we used the Cape Town egg-donor agency, $9,500 if we didn't. Certainly not chump change, but still far less than what we'd pay in the United States. And we'd get a two-week trip to an exotic place we'd never been. We signed up.

Screening Donors

Marty and I could't imagine creating a child with the genes of someone we could't lay eyes on. We both wanted to pay the extra money to use the Cape Town egg-donor agency. I obtained the password for Renew Fertility's online donor database and began poring over pictures and background information on dozens of young women. Most of them, I learned, were donating eggs for altruistic reasons, as the South African government limits donors' compensation to 5,000 rand, or about $700. That's not much money, considering what's involved for the donors. They inject fertility drugs to produce multiple eggs, then undergo a surgical procedure to have the eggs removed from their ovaries.

One day our donor's picture—a new recruit with unproven eggs—popped up on the Web site. She looked nothing like me. A blonde, while I am a brunette. Thin, angular features; I have full lips and bulgy eyes. But still, there was something about her that appealed to me. A kindness in her eyes? An intelligence? She was getting her master's degree in an outdoorsy field that could land her on Animal Planet one day. She also had curly hair—something I had become very sad about not being able to pass on. And she was twenty-two and oh-so-healthy. I was smitten. Marty liked her, too. We wrote her the letter that was required by the donor agency. We told her our story and waited for her answer, knowing that this would be our last high-priced attempt at pregnancy—the end of a long odyssey, no matter the outcome.

A few days later, we heard back from the agency. She'd said yes to becoming our donor. Yes, also, to meeting us while we were in Cape Town. We were on our way.

A Second Option

That's when the phone rang and our long quest for a baby took an unexpected turn. It was Marty's cousin, an obstetrician in South Carolina who'd been following our conception difficulties.

"I might have a baby for you," she announced. "Are you interested?"

"Um . . . what?" I sputtered.

A young woman had come into her practice. She was fourteen weeks along and wanted to place the baby for adoption. The father, nineteen, was not in the picture, and the birth mother—a cute, healthy,—twenty-three-year-old named Laney who worked in a restaurant and still lived with her mom—did not want to be a single parent. She was willing to place the baby privately with a couple like Marty and me. Were we in? Could we get a home study done really quickly?

"Um . . . what?" I just kept saying.

Having It Both Ways

Adoption was not something I'd wanted to do. In fact, for years, I was wholly unable to picture it. One day, you are most decidedly not a parent, and then the next day you are? How was I supposed to wrap my head around that? Plus, something deep within me wanted to be pregnant—needed to be pregnant. Badly. Just once. I could see adopting later. But not now.

And yet, when our third IVF attempt had failed, and Marty and I had sat there on the couch stunned, staring blankly at the home pregnancy test with just one sorry, stupid line on it, we decided to open the door to all possibilities, to all ways to be a family. Adoption was one of those ways.

I called Marty, then called his cousin right back. "Yes, yes, we're in," I told her.

We'd do both, Marty and I decided. We'd hedge our bets, pursuing both this adoption (which could be done without an agency and, thus, inexpensively) and the donor-egg cycle in South Africa. If the adoption fell through—and they often do, we were told—we'd still have the donor cycle. If the donor cycle didn't work, we'd still have the adoption under way. The baby in South Carolina was due July 22, 2006, six weeks after our scheduled return from Cape Town. Should all efforts be successful, we'd have two babies, spaced seven months apart.

Or, um, three babies, should the South Africa experience result in twins, as many IVF cycles do. I took a deep breath, then laughed. Two babies? Maybe three? After this huge drought? Were we in?

Yes, definitely. . . .

Arriving in South Africa

I stumbled down the gangway in Johannesburg puking into an airline-issued vomit bag. I guess it was the Ambien I'd taken to help me sleep on our eighteen-hour sojourn from Washington to South Africa. Or maybe it was all the estrogen

I was taking to prepare my uterus to house the embryos that would be forming in a few days. But I couldn't help thinking of my uncharacteristic retching as a good omen. Was the universe telling me that, in a few weeks, I might get to vomit even more? Because that's what I wanted. Morning sickness and lots of it.

The morning after our arrival in Cape Town, we climbed into a cab, eager for our first meeting with Paul le Roux. When the cab pulled up to his address, we saw a giant Pic 'n Pay grocery store with an office building above it. A fertility clinic and a grocery store sharing space? Was there some mistake? No, there wasn't.

On the second floor of the office building, we found le Roux nestled in a modest office. He was thin, wearing a sweater vest. He welcomed us warmly, asking about our flights and seeming to care about the answers. He had a nature just as nurturing as I'd been promised. Maybe that's why the bad news he delivered didn't hit me that hard at first.

Discouraging News

"I'm so sorry to say the donor"—whom we were scheduled to meet the following week—"hasn't produced very many ee-eeeggs," le Roux told us from across his desk. "There are only four or five right now, with a few more that may catch up."

Bad news, indeed. In the United States, doctors tend to prescribe high doses of fertility drugs to donors causing them to produce, say, maybe fifteen eggs on the low end and maybe thirty-five on the very high end. That way, couples have a lot of eggs to work with and, perhaps, some embryos to freeze to create future children. In South Africa, we learned, they keep the drug doses lower, believing that it's safer for the donor. And getting, say, ten eggs from a donor is a good thing there. We were okay with that. But four or five eggs?

Le Roux also told us the donor's eggs were developing faster than normal—another possible sign of compromised fertility—and that they were being surgically removed the following day. Could we be there at 9 A.M the next morning so Marty could produce the necessary sperm?

After we agreed, the doctor had me hop up onto an ultrasound table so he could check the thickness of my uterine lining. It was a healthy and embryo-ready 10.5 mm [millimeters]. That was the visit's only uplifting news. But I decided I wasn't going to freak out. After all, if things didn't work out here, we had the adoption to fall back on, right? And I was going to enjoy this vacation no matter what happened, dammit. . . .

A Backup Donor

The next day, we were halfway through lunch at one of the wineries outside cape town when our cellphone rang. It was le Roux. Marty took the call. I tried to read his face as le Roux talked, but all I could pick up was utter confusion.

"Here, let me let you talk to Suz," was all Marty said.

Le Roux said: "Suz, hello, yes. I'm calling because it seems that, out of the four eggs we got yesterday from the donor, only two were mature. Both of those have fertilized, but I'm concerned. Two is not really enough to work with."

I felt an uncomfortable heat spread across my middle, and then suddenly all my viscera seemed to be dropping fast, as if I were on a roller coaster that had just rounded the top of its worst dip. But there wasn't time to say anything before le Roux swooped in with a possible fix. It seemed that, coincidentally, he had another donor, one who was ready to have her eggs extracted in a few hours, and her recipient couple had canceled at the last moment. She, too, had a small batch of eggs coming along—maybe five or six. Would we like to have her eggs as backup? At no extra cost?

My stomach stopped dropping. The roller coaster hung in midair. Le Roux was the man.

"Uh, what is she like?" I asked.

"Oh! Quite nice!" le Roux gushed. She was one of his favorite donors, he said, with coloring more similar to mine. He
could show us a childhood picture if we came in, he said. This
donor was 28, very sweet, worked in computers. She was pretty
and fit, maybe a bit taller than me. She had donated twice before, and pregnancies had occurred both times—one of which
resulted in twins.

In an instant, Marty and I found ourselves saying yes.
Never mind all our careful combing over donor pictures and
profile info before coming here, painstakingly considering the
genes we would carry forth into a new generation. Never
mind that it felt as though we were cheating on our original
donor, whom we'd be meeting soon. This called for a snap decision, and we made it. . . .

Choosing the Embryos

Flash forward three days: now we had to choose which embryos to use. It's standard practice when using an egg donor
to transfer two embryos to the uterus. More than that and
you risk triplets; fewer than that and you risk no pregnancy at
all. But should we use the two most robust-looking ones, even
if they were from two different donors? What if I ended up
with twins, then, with different biological mothers? Le Roux
said he worried that could be difficult to explain to the children.

That made sense to us. Plus, we knew the second donor's
eggs had produced nothing but pregnancies. "We'll go with
the two best from donor No. 2's batch," we said. "And we'll
freeze the rest."

Le Roux wheeled in his ultrasound machine. I lay flat on
the exam table. Marty held my hand. The embryologist came
in with the embryos loaded into a syringe. Le Roux fed a
catheter through my cervix and up into the uterus, watching
the whole thing on a screen to get the positioning right.

Finally, he pushed the embryos through the apparatus and into me. A bright little flash appeared at the end of the catheter.

Life! Well, maybe. We wouldn't know for ten days.

A Difficult Meeting

We pulled into the parking lot of a Cape Town restaurant with a quaking nervousness. Did we have to do this? What was the point of meeting our original donor now? It was too late, though, to back out.

"You go first," Marty said as we walked toward the restaurant.

"No—you."

"No—you," he urged, half-kidding, half-not.

I crossed the gravel courtyard beyond the restaurant's bar, and then I saw her about fifty feet away, sitting on one end of a picnic-table bench. I recognized her from pictures on the Web site. We introduced ourselves. She radiated a remarkable sincerity and was far more beautiful than her pictures let on. She had big, round, gorgeous green eyes, and her hair was the exact texture of mine—fine and curly-wavy, bordering on frizzy, only blond.

An Exchange of Gifts

Shyly, looking at the table, she said she was so sorry her donation to us hadn't worked out. I told her not to worry. I gave her the present we'd brought for her—a tent, which she needed for her fieldwork. It's customary to give the donors here a fairly expensive gift, because the government prohibits them from getting much in the way of a donor fee.

We asked her about her work, and she regaled us with details about her time spent deep in the bush. She was wonderfulf—exactly the sort of young woman you'd want to replace your genetic material with. I started to get a sinking feeling.

When we all stood to leave, she gave me a present wrapped in opalescent paper. A present? For us? I'd never heard of a donor giving the recipient couple a present—only the other way around. I thanked her profusely, without opening it. My sinking feeling deepened.

In the car, I opened the present. It was a copy of [author] Rudyard Kipling's *Just So Stories*, a collection of sassy, fanciful tales about how various jungle animals came to have their traits—how the leopard got his spots, how the elephant got his trunk. "This book was read to me over and over as a child," her card said. It also said, "Thank you for allowing me to share in such a wondrous process of creation. To you and your baby to be, all my love. . ."

Disappointments

The flight home was worse than the flight to South Africa. The excitement was over. And my peanut-oil-filled butt made it impossible to get comfortable. I spent the better part of twenty hours shifting from one cheek to the other.

Three days after we arrived home, I stood in my bathroom with a home pregnancy test. I'd been here so many times before, each one filled with a mixture of anxiety and hope. Marty waited outside the door. When I was done, he came in. We hugged as we waited the obligatory three minutes. When it was time, I broke loose and picked up the stick.

Not pregnant.

My legs suddenly wouldn't hold me. I sank down onto the toilet seat in total disbelief. "No," I said, thinking there just had to be a mistake.

"How?" Marty demanded. "How? After everything we did? After going this far? How? Why?"

"No," I said again, staring at the side of the tub.

The next day an official blood test at my old IVF clinic's office in Annandale confirmed the results: We weren't having a baby.

A Different Path

In a Charleston, S.C., courtroom two weeks later, Laney waddled to the witness stand. She was so heavy with child that I was afraid she'd topple off her black platform sandals.

Marty and I watched nervously as she raised her right hand and swore to tell the whole truth. Our lawyer had assured us that this particular adoption proceeding was just a formality. And, through phone calls and e-mails, Laney still seemed resolute about the fate of her baby.

"Is it your intention to place your baby with this couple?" said the lawyer, motioning to us.

"Yes, sir," Laney answered.

"When is the baby due?"

"In a month, sir."

"You feel that it is in the best interest of the child to be placed with this couple?"

"I do, sir."

The prospect of this adoption was allowing Marty and me to stave off complete despair. "Marty, let's call her Evangeline Virginia," I'd said to him not long after the devastating pregnancy test. "Evangeline after the [Henry Wadsworth] Longfellow poem, and Virginia after your grandmother. Then we can just call her Eve for short."

"I love it," Marty had said.

We still weren't entirely confident that Laney would hand us her baby and make us parents. All we could do was hope. It's all we'd ever done.

On July 25, the day Laney was being induced by Marty's cousin's partner, we sat in the hospital waiting room with Laney's relatives and three of her best friends. The initial awkwardness disappeared quickly. Over the course of the next 12 hours, we played cards, asked about each other's work, took bets on how much the baby would weigh. Laney's dad gave us some children's books he'd illustrated. Her cousin, an aspiring artist, showed me her work on a Web site. They embraced us as family, which felt right. After all, this was to be an open adoption, and in a matter of hours—if all went as planned—we'd be linked forever.

Laney's labor seemed to take forever. The double doors didn't fly open until 10:30 P.M., when Laney's shellshocked-looking aunt, who along with Laney's mom had been there for the birth, announced the news: The baby was here, but she was in some distress. She had been born face-up, the cord wrapped around her neck. Her arm had come out next to her face, and she had a fever and jaundice. She would probably be fine but needed to be watched closely. Laney, we were told, was exhausted but doing well. Her aunt then collapsed in a corner.

Marty and I were the last to be called in to see Laney that night. It was 1:30 A.M., and the baby had just been placed in Laney's arms after hours and hours of testing. She was beautiful, with wide-set eyes, a gorgeous nose and porcelain baby doll skin. I'd gotten her a onesie that said "Movie Star," and it seemed apt. Laney held tight to her. We fussed over the two of them, wondering when Laney was going to pass the baby to us for a few minutes. But she never did.

"I'm sorry. I can't. Not yet. I'm sorry," she said, on the verge of tears.

Marty rose to the occasion immediately. "Okay, sure—we understand. Whatever you need to do. Whatever makes you comfortable."

I started to feel pressure mounting in my head like a kinked hose on full blast. I held it all back until we got in the car. Then I sobbed and ranted. What did it mean? Was Laney keeping the baby? Was this all for naught, too? What the hell had we done to deserve all this?

We slept a few hours, then woke and showered, moving around heavily as we got ready to head back to the hospital. As I pulled on my shirt, my cell rang. It was Laney. She sounded completely different—cheery.

"Hey! Are you guys coming? We've pulled a rocker in here for you to sit and feed the baby. Come on over and start bonding with Eve. We can't wait to see you. Come be with your baby!"

"What did she say?" Marty asked me after I hung up.

I couldn't answer. All I could do was cry.

New Beginnings

It is Halloween night. Eve has just turned three months old. I parade her up and down the block in our Falls Church neighborhood, thrilled to participate, for the first time, in this parental ritual that had always eluded me. We have a baby. And here she is, dressed up as a chicken. Neighbors coo. Passersby swoon. But no one admires her as much as I do. She is everything we could have wanted—healthy, sweet, mild-mannered and, yet, feisty, curious, smiley. She has the eyes of an old soul.

With Eve's arrival, my visceral desire for pregnancy has vanished. When I see pregnant women now, I no longer feel the painful tug that was with me for so long. Instead, I find myself thinking: Man, that seems like a pain in the ass. And then I look at my baby, and she lights up, legs kicking involuntarily from delight, blue eyes sparkling.

The other day, when I handed Eve to a friend, the baby started to cry. Perplexing, I thought. She just ate. She just napped. She's not a big sobber. What gives? Then the same thing happened a few nights later when we handed her to Marty's aunt. Sob, sob, sob. What's this? we puzzled. But when I took her back into my arms, she quieted right down. Then I understood: She wants only to be held by us; we're her parents.

Choosing Surrogacy

Jacquelyn Mitchard

As Jacquelyn Mitchard notes in her essay, surrogacy—the process of a woman carrying and giving birth to a baby for another person—is a solution for infertility that dates back to Biblical times. Modern techniques such as in vitro fertilization and egg donation, however, have catapulted this ancient practice into the twenty-first century. When Mitchard and her second husband, Chris Brent, decided to have a child, Mitchard was already in her forties and seemed unlikely to get pregnant naturally. Although they quickly adopted an infant, they still wanted to have a child that was at least partly biologically theirs.

Surrogacy seemed an attractive option, but, as Mitchard relates in this story, ended up being far more complicated than either she or her husband had anticipated. High fees (which include both the fees paid to the surrogate mother herself as well as to the fertility clinics, physicians, and lawyers involved) make the process prohibitively expensive. High failure rates lend surrogacy the same kind of cyclical disappointments characteristic of other fertility treatments. And, finally, as Mitchard discovered, surrogacy has very real emotional costs for everyone involved and often includes the possibility that the gestational mother will change her mind about turning over the baby to the intended parents.

Although Jacquelyn Mitchard vows at the end of her essay that "I will never walk this road [of surrogacy] again," she and her husband did arrange for another surrogate pregnancy two years after Will's birth. That surrogacy experience was even more fraught with complications than the one Mitchard describes here, resulting in a protracted custody battle involving the gestational mother's husband. In the end, though, Mitchard was able to keep her son, the youngest of seven children.

Jacquelyn Mitchard, "She's Having My Baby," *Parenting*, vol. 18, August 2004. Copyright Time Inc. All rights reserved. Reproduced by permission.

Deciding to have a child via surrogacy was easy. It was the next two years that were wrenching—physically, financially, and emotionally

Well, we wanted a baby. That was the first shocker. When I remarried after five years of widowhood, my new husband, a dozen years younger than I, adopted all four of my children who still lived at home (my eldest daughter is grown). And he couldn't wait to have another child. So after repeated miscarriages—probably due to the cranky quirks of a fortysomething body that had never been very cooperative, fertility-wise—we adopted a baby girl. But we wanted yet one more. And in truth, I didn't want Chris to regret missing the experience of biological parenthood (though he'd never even hinted that this was an issue).

A Casual Suggestion

So when an acquaintance, a nurse at the clinic where, fifteen years before, I'd become pregnant through in vitro fertilization (IVF) made an offhand suggestion, I thought, Eureka! She asked if I'd considered gestational surrogacy, in which an egg, not mine but fertilized by Chris's sperm, would be implanted in a womb, again not mine. In just nine months, we'd have a baby! Talented and lovely egg donors were at the ready, we'd heard. What could be better for us? Surrogacy was nothing new: Even Old Testament Abraham and Sarah took that route. Moral compunctions? None whatsoever. This was hard and serious women's work that deserved fair pay. We knew it involved vulnerable hearts and delicate sensibilities. A designer child conceived in greed and born in hubris? Pshaw. All manner of people have all manner of motives for all manner of things—some good, some shockingly selfish. We knew that ours were decent.

We went in with eyes wide open.

We had no idea how wide our eyes could get.

A Series of Surprises

We had no idea how complex, wrenching, poignant, exhilarating, frustrating, costly, bitter, tender, satisfying, and terrifying would be the long journey that would lead to the birth of our baby, Will. Nor how close we would come to never. We had no idea that we would pay the cost of a small airplane for various high-tech potions and genetic recombinations, only to finally succeed with a syringe meant for giving a baby a dose of medicine, bought at Walgreens for $3.99.

That was three years ago. And we were probably better prepared for the surprises than most couples, having gone through the ups and downs of adoption.

We knew that many surrogates are underemployed or underappreciated, happy for the chance to do something a seemingly more powerful person cannot. We wanted someone who would not turn our desire into a struggle or psychological drama. There are agencies that will "match" couples with surrogates for hefty fees. But good judges of character that we were, we thought we'd find our own. We'd do no worse, we thought, than most people do at choosing spouses.

Striking It Rich or Striking Out?

So we interviewed, oh, ten, fifty, finally about two hundred women, over six months, through a free website called Surro-momsonline.com. Some were wonderful but were in inconvenient locations—like Germany. Some were overly intimate at first e-mail, a red flag or a hungry heart. Some were taken but would get back to us in two years.

Then, gold.

Annie's advertisement made her seem like an old friend: a country gal, mother of four, surrogate mother of one, with a big heart and smarts to match. Combine Annie with Andrea (located through the same site), an intelligent egg donor with (oh, glory!) red hair, and three months and $18,000 later, we were rewarded with four healthy eggs to implant.

No pregnancy.

Second try. Same site, new egg donor—a former Olympic athlete whose resume is graced with an accounting degree, a modeling job, and a history of gestational success. Ten thousand bucks. Annie's ready, willing, and able womb.

No pregnancy.

That, it turns out, was the time to have stopped.

Why didn't we?

Borderline Obsession

Maybe it was because this most wanted of babies was now dancing just beyond our grasp. The word "obsession" comes to mind.

We started prowling websites and Internet mailing lists to scope out the territory and read others' stories. We learned the lingo. "GS" stood for "gestational surrogate," who carried donor eggs fertilized by the sperm of the "IP," or "intended parent." A "TS" (traditional surrogate) was impregnated, usually through "AI" (artificial insemination), thus donating her genetic material as well as carrying the pregnancy herself. This combining of roles often had a greater emotional risk but usually resulted in a less fragile, less medication-dependent pregnancy.

We also got a big, fat reality check. Some couples had re- and remortgaged their homes for just one more IVF try. Some had paid thousands of dollars for medical and psychological tests only to have their surrogates ditch them for couples who'd pay even more. I cyber-chatted with women born without ovaries, who'd survived cancer and kidney transplants, all undeterred by the statistics (only a third of all pregnancy attempts succeed). Some couples so adored their surrogates, they'd made them godparents of the babies they'd helped create. Others never spoke to each other again after delivery. One surro-mom became so attached to the family for whom she'd borne a child that six months after their son was born, she sent them a "certificate for a sibling"—free of charge.

We read of a London surrogate who said she was pregnant with twins for a San Francisco–area couple who didn't want two and demanded she abort one. In general, however, we found that most folks on both sides of the ledger were reasonable people with high hopes, strained emotions, and understandable fears.

Trying Again

Meanwhile, we decided to try TS. We found Elise through a site IPs join for a small fee, IntendedParents.com. Then her boyfriend confessed his "discomfort" and said if our try worked, he would insist on abortion.

It didn't.

Back to Surromomsonline and Marie, the next potential surrogate. She said she'd be glad to work with us, but not right now because she was pregnant with triplets; she was angry when we would not put down a deposit and wait for a year. Next we found Kayley, who did exclusively TS, so my husband flew five states away for a try. He still can't talk about how it felt to be jammed into a minuscule bathroom in their house, trying to "donate" with only a thin wall between him and the La-Z-Boy where her husband was watching football. Though a sultry brunette in her photo, Kayley turned out to be a painfully thin blonde in person, who wasn't even sure she'd ovulated. When she offered us another try, we declined.

By now, we were out of whatever disposable savings we'd accumulated and well into the lean financial tissue of our lives.

But then my magnificent friend Natalie said she'd like to help, to donate her eggs. After two months and 20 shots in Nattie's slender hip, five perfect eggs were implanted in Jenna, who lived just an hour south of our home and who'd actually found us after reading our ad on the IntendedParents site. She lived on a farm with her Amish husband and their four kids.

Three weeks later, we saw the blue line.

Three weeks after that, we saw our little baby's strong heartbeat! The nurse told us that more than 90 percent of fetuses with heartbeats that strong went all the way to term.

Three weeks after that, it stopped.

And so did we. Forever, we said.

That lasted a week.

Back to Basics

It was Chris who chose Gracie, a new face on a new website, one that no longer exists, a mom whose dedication to becoming a surrogate was so complete she'd already completed her "P and P's" (psychological and physical tests). Cheerful and sweet, she had an adorable Southern accent on the telephone, and, in photos, she had a "kissy" mouth with which I fell in love. We had three frozen eggs left from our previous attempts, but frozen eggs have a lesser chance to "take."

And at this point a lesser chance of success was more than we could bear.

So we opted for traditional surrogacy. Real traditional. As in "turkey-baster" traditional.

Two months, a few STD tests, and a paper flurry later, Gracie and her daughter, Cullen, 2, were guests in our spare room. After an office confab with our longtime friend, a family-practice doctor, I carried a Walgreen's medical syringe filled with Chris's reproductive contribution down the hall to her. Three weeks after we hugged Gracie and Cullen goodbye, another blue line, then another heartbeat. . .and then, after five months of daily e-mail, weekly phone calls, and two visits, we watched a nurse put gel on Gracie's growing belly and skate a monitor over the gently shifting mound. Then we saw—full face and seemingly happy to see us—our son.

Gracie said, "Go ahead, Chris. It's okay to cry."

Unwelcome Developments

Six weeks before Will's due date, Gracie began to have early contractions. Because we'd planned the birth to take place in our city, she flew the thousand miles to us, her father escorting her. He was not all smiles. Angry at all the medication Gracie had had to take to stop the contractions, he thought what his little girl was enduring was unfair. This would not change.

But something else did.

Two weeks after Gracie arrived, on the anniversary of my late husband's death from colon cancer, my mammogram detected a lump in my breast—not a cyst, a lump. A biopsy was scheduled for, oh, two weeks from next Tuesday.

Feeling I'd coaxed fate too far by dint of my greed, I wept and railed and took to bed. Finally, a friend called another friend, who did us a favor and scheduled my biopsy for 7 A.M. the next morning. Two days after that, I found out that sometimes a lump is just a lump.

My Worst Fears

But my histrionics had terrified Gracie. Now that her contractions had settled down, she wanted to go home. As she left, she asked me, "Is there any way they can test the blood of the fetus to make sure the baby is really Chris's?"

I was dumbfounded.

She added, "It has to be, but just to be sure."

"You . . . have doubts that the baby was conceived by Chris?"

"Not really. I just want to be sure. . ."

The next two weeks were not my finest 288 hours. I should have had duct tape placed over my mouth and keyboard. Then an icy note came from Gracie's dad, asking me to give her space. It squeezed my heart like a frozen rubber glove.

At my sternum, a devil tapped. Gracie was not going to give our baby to us.

And we could not force her to because under law, despite the contract stating that this child was being created to be the offspring of Chris and me, even if Gracie allowed genetic tests after the birth, the presumptive father of any baby born to any married women is that woman's husband. A day later, a note from Gracie's husband, Ray, informed us that Gracie would be giving birth at her own hometown hospital, with her own doctor.

If I could have had myself committed at that point, I might have.

Fearful she would end up going into labor with what seemed to be a large baby and preferring to deliver via a C-section, Gracie scheduled the baby's birth for three weeks before the due date.

Hurtful Words

With three of our children in tow, we hastily traveled down the length of the country to join them. The moment I saw Gracie, all the sharp words dissolved into a cotton-candy cloud. We all ate fish gumbo together and laughed long. At 5 A.M., when Gracie was wheeled into surgery, I was the one she chose to accompany her. And at 8:07 A.M. on the seventh day of the eighth month, the photos of me, in my paper surgical scrubs, with 8-pound 11-ounce William Gordon Pendragon Brent (my husband's last name) in my arms, are as close to anything I've ever seen of a middle-aged woman blissed out on drugs.

Gracie wanted to care for Will in the hospital. Her father phoned her aunts and grandparents. That same day, the genetic tests, scrapings of Will's, Chris's, and Ray's cheeks, returned. Of 99.8 percent of all sperm donors, Chris was the most likely biological dad. That night, moved to heartbreak by Gracie's physical pain and emotional turmoil, I told her and her dad, "This has to be so hard. I wish there were two little Wills, one for you and one for me. I hate feeling like I'm hurting you."

The next day Gracie said, "Please, I know you mean it when you say you don't want me to hurt anymore. So you take your kids home. And I'll take Will home." She'd name him Malory.

Doing the Right Thing

The next forty-eight hours are a red-eyed blur in my memory, but I can say this: Never was I more grateful to have married a graceful man. With me and the children huddled in the hospital cafeteria, Chris watched silently as Ray and Gracie struggled together, Ray insisting that they had no choice but to keep their part of the bargain, Gracie insisting she could not.

Finally intervening, Chris turned and looked into Gracie's great gray eyes—the very same eyes into which I look every day, when I lean over my gigantic, gorgeous, giggly blond baby boy's crib. "You know what's right, Gracie, and you want to do it," he said.

And so, the next morning, she did.

She put Will into Chris's arms. And then we held Gracie, who confessed that she had never, ever imagined—never—how wrenching an experience this would be. I melted. When I told her she was a better woman than I, a hero, it might have sounded like blarney, meant to get us out of that hospital room and out of Dodge.

But I meant it.

Immeasurable Costs

There were times we felt we ought to have been paid for going through surrogacy. And there were times we felt that what we paid, emotionally and economically, was beggared by the haloed, hallowed result: our beloved boy. Like many hard-won kids, he was born happy, quickly slept through the night, guzzled quarts of formula, and has never even had a diaper rash.

Gracie healed quickly, got pregnant, and suffered an early miscarriage. But soon she recovered from that and was expecting again.

Are we friends?

No. We are both less, and more.

At Will's baptism, Gracie will not be among the guests. That would hurt her too much. But sometimes, during our less and less frequent emails, I call her "Little Sis." Too late, I realized that was what Gracie had needed—a grown-up, serene, all-knowing, and approving sib, not the basket case I was by the time we met. She deserved a gentler hand. And yet she and I—two high-strung hot reactors—have made a peace hardened in the fire.

She is in Will. When a look crosses his face that is pure Gracie, I love that look. Pictures of Gracie dot Will's baby book. There will be no attempt to erase her. I'll never forget her. I'll never regret her.

And I will never walk this road again.

Nobody Has the Right
to Be a Mother

Amanda Platell

Coming to terms with childlessness is a fact of life for many in-fertile couples. In vitro attempts can fail (or be too costly), adoption hopes can fall through, and eventually many couples must learn to live with the knowledge that parenthood is just not feasible. Amanda Platell is one of those who has come to terms with her own childlessness, not willingly or easily, but with her own brand of common sense. A high-achieving career woman, Platell is outraged when acquaintances assume that she simply "forgot to have children" while pursuing her professional success. In fact, although she rarely talks about it openly, Platell admits that her failure to have children is a major source of disappointment for her.

She expresses scorn at the notion, perpetuated by the popularity of new fertility treatments, that every woman is entitled to experience motherhood. In fact, Platell argues, some women are destined never to be mothers but rather to be, for example, favorite aunts instead. This is a role Platell has embraced whole-heartedly in her own life, and one that has helped her come to terms with her inability to have children.

Amanda Platell is a native of Australia but has lived in the United Kingdom (UK) since the 1980s. A longtime journalist and former press secretary to William Hague, a leader of Britain's Conservative Party, Platell now hosts a political interview show on the British television station Channel 4.

One of the things I regret about my early career in newspapers is a big poster I had on my office wall when I was deputy editor of [UK newspaper] *today*. It was one of those

1950s cartoons of a glamorous brunette, with a speech bubble saving: "I can't believe I forgot to have children."

I regret it because I think it reinforced a myth that career women do forget about babies—until it's too late. And for me, nothing could have been further from the truth. I didn't forget. For me, children were just never one of life's gifts.

An Inalienable Right?

I thought about that poster the other day when I heard Suzi Leather, the chair of the Human Fertilisation and Embryology Authority, calling for a change in the law to make it easier for single and gay women to get fertility treatment. It triggered the usual debate on the role of fathers in families. What it also did was imply that, with modern treatments, all women can have kids. Somehow the right to be a mother has become inalienable.

I know from experience that a woman has about as much right to motherhood as she has to happiness. It's neither a right nor an obligation, but the current debate swirling around Leather's comments seems to suggest both.

The implication behind a change of law that gives every woman, whatever her circumstances, the right to fertility treatment is that there is an obligation to take it up. That being a mother is the be-all and end-all of a woman's existence.

Not My Choice

I don't think I'm being oversenstive. I've spent my life with people assuming that l placed ambition above motherhood, that my career was more important than a child. It's a cruel assumption, and one that many succcssful, childless career women suffer in silence. I only know this because I recently made a throwaway comment on *Woman's Hour*, saying that people assume I chose not to have kids but it was one of the great tragedies of my life that I couldn't. I've lost count of the women who phoned or e-mailed or simply came up to me and said: "Thank you for saying that."

There are lots of us about. A quarter of forty-year-old women in this country don't have kids. You'd be making a big mistake if you assumed that this was by choice. As did one woman I had just met. She asked if I regretted not having kids, as if I had a choice in the matter. I said, as it happens, I couldn't. She replied: "There are lots of different ways of being a mother, you know. You can have IVF or donor eggs, or you can adopt."

Finding Fulfillment

Well, call me selfish, but I only ever wanted to be a mother one way, with my own child born into a loving relationship with its father. I never thought that being a mother was just about my fulfillment.

I hope I'm living proof that a woman can have a fulfilled and worthwhile life without children; that there is love to be got and given. Recently I was discussing this with my sister-in-law, Ingrid, a doctor and the mother of three terrific kids. "It's great being a mum," she said, "but you end up being defined in terms of that. You, on the other hand, have been able to fulfil yourself as a woman. You're not defined in terms of any-one else."

Well, I guess that's true, but I also know that if God came down right now, sat beside me and offered to change one thing about my life, it would be that I could have had chil-dren. No, that's not true, my first wish would be that my brother Michael had not died. But my second wish. . . .

What Childlessness Means

And at least one person is glad about it all. Ingrid's eldest daughter and my niece, Ariane, says: "I don't ever want you to have kids, Auntie Mandy, because then you'd love me less." And love her I do, with a passion, as I do all my five nieces and nephews. Being childless doesn't mean being loveless or unloved. But it does mean you have to work harder on those relationships. No love is your due when you are but aunt or friend.

I suppose what really worries me about the stand Leather takes is that while it proclaims it is the right of every infertile woman to have fertility treatment, it also implies, ever so subtly, that there's something wrong with a woman who doesn't go down that path. Something wrong with a woman who chooses not to have IVF, with its 75 percent failure rate and still largely unknown long-term effects on both mother and baby. Something wrong with a woman who, if her own eggs or her partner's sperm aren't up to the job, chooses not to carry a stranger's egg or a stranger's sperm and, consequently, a stranger's baby. Something wrong with a woman who chooses not to have a baby without a father.

New Definitions

One of the reasons I have spoken so little about this is that I never wanted to be defined in terms of my childlessness. Nor have I ever thought of myself as being blissfully child-free, as some women happily do, and good luck to them. But the truth is, not being able to have kids has not defined me, but it has defined my life.

I'm just a girl who grew up dreaming that one day she'd be married—hopefully to that nice Alan Drake-Brockman (the only double-barrelled family in Applecross)—and have a houseful of kids. And when finally, I discovered that there would be no houseful of kids, I tried to make the best of what I had. And I've had a lot.

The last word will go to my 13-year-old niece, Ariane: "Ok u r different coz u don't have children, but that doesn't mean that's a bad thing, coz i tork to u bout stuff which i wudn't tork to mum about and u cum and do r hair and put on make up and stuff and take us shopping and we tell u every-thing. we're ur children at heart, so i guess ur like a kool aun-tie mandy mum person."

A cool Auntie Mandy Mum person—yes, that sounds like a fine thing to me.

Organizations to Contact

The editors have compiled the following list of organizations concerned with the issues debated in this book. The descriptions are derived from materials provided by the organizations. All have publications or information available for interested readers. The list was compiled on the date of publication of the present volume; the information provided here may change. Be aware that many organizations take several weeks or longer to respond to inquiries, so allow as much time as possible.

American Fertility Association(AFA)
666 Fifth Avenue, Suite 278, New York, NY   10103
(888) 917-3777 • fax: (718) 601-7722
e-mail: info@theafa.org
Web site: www.theafa.org

The American Fertility Association (AFA) is a national non-profit organization whose mission focuses on "educating, supporting, and advocating for men and women concerned with reproductive health, fertility preservation, infertility and all forms of family building." The AFA's Web site hosts occasional online forums, several message boards covering many aspects of fertility, links to support groups and therapists, and many informational articles. The AFA also sponsors in-person workshops and publishes a magazine *(InFocus)* and several newsletters (free online registration required).

American Pregnancy Association (APA)
1425 Greenway Drive, Suite 440, Irving, TX   75038
(800) 672-2296 • fax: (972) 550-0140
e-mail: Questions@AmericanPregnancy.org
Web site: www.americanpregnancy.org

The American Pregnancy Association (APA) is a nonprofit organization committed to providing information about pregnancy to the general public. The APA maintains a Web site with facts about all aspects of pregnancy as well as related topics such as fertility, birth defects, and adoption. In addition, the APA's toll-free helpline is available as a resource for people with questions about pregnancy.

American Society for Reproductive Medicine (ASRM)
1209 Montgomery Highway, Birmingham, AL   35216-2809
(205) 978-5000 • fax: (205) 978-5005
e-mail: asrm@asrm.org
Web site: www.asrm.org

Made up of fertility experts from all fifty states and more than a hundred other countries, the American Society for Reproductive Medicine is a professional organization whose members contribute to educational and advocacy efforts related to fertility issues. The Society's official publication, *Fertility and Sterility*, is a peer-reviewed professional medical journal. It also publishes several newsletters for its member physicians as well as an array of patient information booklets. For patients, the ASRM's Web site offers lists of frequently asked questions, information about insurance coverage for medical procedures, and links to physicians..

The Endometriosis Association
8585 N. 76th Place, Milwaukee, WI   53223
(414) 355-2200 • fax: (414) 355-6065
Web site: www.endo-online.org

Endometriosis, a common condition in which endometrial tissue grows outside a woman's uterus, is one of the leading causes of female infertility. The Endometriosis Association's Web site includes an interactive diagnostic tool, descriptions of treatment options, and links to endometriosis support groups. In addition to a free informational packet (available through the Web site), the association publishes books such as *The Endometriosis Sourcebook* and *Endometriosis: A Key to Healing Through Nutrition*.

Fertile Hope
PO Box 624, New York, NY 10014
(888) 994-HOPE • fax: (888) 994-HOPE
e-mail: feedback@fertilehope.org
Web site: www.fertilehope.org

Infertility can be one of the side effects faced by people undergoing cancer treatment. Fertile Hope provides information
and resources to these cancer patients through education, financial assistance, research, and support. Fertile Hope's Web
site offers a searchable health care provider directory, a list of
frequently asked questions, links to sources of financial aid,
and a message board.

International Council on Infertility
Information Dissemination (INCIID)
PO BOX 6836, Arlington, VA 22206
(703) 379-9178 • fax: (703) 379-1593
e-mail: inciidinfo@inciid.org
Web site: www.inciid.org

The International Council on Infertility Information Dissemi-
nation (INCIID, pronounced "inside") "provides current information and immediate support regarding the diagnosis,
treatment, and prevention of infertility and pregnancy loss,
and offers guidance to those considering adoption or childfree
lifestyles." INCIID's Web site provides numerous articles on
infertility, reproductive technologies, miscarriage, adoption,
insurance, and the law as well as national listings of health
care providers. The nonprofit organization also sponsors an in
vitro fertilization (IVF) scholarship fund for financially quali-
fied couples and publishes an online newsletter, "INCIID In-
sights."

National Infertility Network Exchange (NINE)
c/o Ilene Stargot, Pres., PO Box 204
East Meadow, NY 11554
(516) 794-5772 • fax: (516) 794-0008

e-mail: info@nine-infertility.org
Web site: www.nine-infertility.org

Formed in 1988, the National Infertility Network Exchange (NINE) connects infertile couples through workshops, support groups, and contact lists. In addition, NINE offers its members referrals to physicians and counselors specializing in reproductive issues. NINE publishes a bimonthly newsletter as well as books, fact sheets, and pamphlets. Its Web site includes links to other online resources.

The Organization of Parents Through Surrogacy (OPTS)
PO Box 611, Gurnee, IL   60031
(847) 782-0224
e-mail: bzager@msn.com
Web site: www.opts.com

The Organization of Parents Through Surrogacy (OPTS) is a national nonprofit organization made up of parents, potential parents, surrogate mothers, and professionals who work in the field of infertility. They provide a volunteer network that offers advice and information for couples and potential surrogates who are exploring surrogacy as an option. Their Web site includes free classified listings, a listserv that connects members, a directory of professional services across the country, and several online articles by and for those involved in the surrogacy process.

RESOLVE: The National Infertility Association
7910 Woodmont Ave., Ste. 1350, Bethesda, MD   20814
(301) 652-8585 • fax: (301) 652-9375
e-mail: info@resolve.org
Web site: www.resolve.org

Established in 1974, RESOLVE provides support for people experiencing infertility and increases awareness of fertility issues through education and advocacy campaigns. Dozens of support groups, workshops, education programs, and other events around the country are sponsored by RESOLVE's local and regional affiliates. RESOLVE's publications include the quarterly magazine *Family Building* and the book *Resolving Infertility* as well as fact sheets.

Web Sites
http://www.womenshealth.gov/faq/infertility.htm

This section of the Department of Health and Human Services womenshealth.gov Web site focuses on questions, answers, and statistics related to infertility. It also provides links to other government and nonprofit sources of information and support.

MedlinePlus: Infertility
http://www.nlm.nih.gov/medlineplus/infertility.html

Sponsored by the National Library of Medicine, MedlinePlus is a consumer health information Web site. The section about infertility leads readers to information about basic diagnosis and treatment, sources of support, current research, and organizations. It also provides facts and figures as well as information on clinical trials.

For Further Research

Books

Karen E. Bender and Nina De Gramont (eds.), *Choice: True Stories of Birth, Contraception, Infertility, Adoption, Single Parenthood, and Abortion*. San Francisco: MacAdam Cage, 2007.

Jason Davis, *Baby Steps: A Bloke's-Eye View of IVF*. St. Leonards. NSW, Australia: Allen & Unwin, 2007.

Martina Devlin, *The Hollow Heart: The True Story of How One Woman's Desire to Have a Baby Almost Destroyed Her Life*. New York: Penguin, 2006.

Harry Fisch, *The Male Biological Clock: The Startling News about Aging, Sexuality, and Fertility in Men*. New York: Free Press, 2005.

Caroline Gallup, *Making Babies the Hard Way: Living with Infertility and Treatment*. Philadelphia: Jessica Kingsley, 2007.

Julia Indichova, *Inconceivable: A Woman's Triumph over Despair and Statistics*. New York: Broadway, 2001.

Janet Jaffe, Martha Ourieff Diamond, and David J. Diamond, *Unsung Lullabies: Understanding and Coping with Infertility*. New York: St. Martin's Griffin, 2005.

Beth Kohl, *Embryo Culture: Making Babies in the Twenty-First Century*. New York: Farrar, Straus & Giroux, 2007.

Liza Mundy, *Everything Conceivable: How Assisted Reproduction Is Changing Men, Women, and the World*. New York: Knopf, 2007.

Peggy Orenstein, *Waiting for Daisy*. New York: Bloomsbury, 2007.

Sherry Sontag, *One in a Million: The Real Story of IVF and the Fight to Forge a Family.* New York: PublicAffairs, 2007.

Debora L. Spar, *The Baby Business: How Money, Science, and Politics Drive the Commerce of Conception.* Boston: Harvard Business School Press, 2006.

Julie Vargo and Maureen Regan, *A Few Good Eggs: Two Chicks Dish on Overcoming the Insanity of Infertility.* New York: ReganBooks, 2006.

Periodicals

Brian Alexander, "How Far Would You Go to Have a Baby?" *Glamour*, May 2005.

Anne Burnett, "On Fertile Ground," *Delicious Living*, October 2006.

Joan Caplin, "Baby or Bust," *Money*, May 2006.

Kevin Chappell, "The Male Biological Clock: Is Time Running Out for You?" *Ebony*, June 2005.

Patricia Edmonds, "Making Babies," *Washingtonian*, December 2004.

Lise Funderburg, "Beyond Conceiving," *Prevention*, April 2007.

Melanie Haiken, "Baby? Maybe," *Health*, November 2006.

Lynn Harris, "Infertile in a Baby-Crazed World," *Glamour*, September 2006.

Deborah Kotz, "Success at Last," *U.S. News & World Report*, May 7, 2007

Michelle Meadows, "Facing Infertility," *FDA Consumer*, November–December 2004.

Anna Mulrine, "Making Babies," *U.S. News & World Report*, September 27, 2004.

Lori Oliwenstein, "On Fertile Ground," *Psychology Today*, November–December 2005.

Peggy Orenstein, "Baby Lust," *The New York Times Magazine*, April 1, 2007.

Colleen Parker, "I Gave My Eggs to Another Woman," *Parents*, March 2005.

Gretchen Reynolds, "Will We Grow Babies Outside Their Mothers' Bodies?" *Popular Science*, September 2005.

Tracey Robinson-English, "Infertility: Help for Couples Trying to Conceive," *Ebony*, August 2005.

Barbara Seaman, "Is This Any Way to Have a Baby?" *O: The Oprah Magazine*, February 2004.

Melissa Schorr, "How Fertile Are You?" *Working Mother*, July–August 2004.

Linda Villarosa, "Baby Hunger," *Essence*, April 2004.

Geoff Williams, "What a Man!" *Baby Talk*, October 2006.

Index